Jam' n Java
For the Soul

Jam'n Java
For the Soul
Book One

Written By
Pastor Chuck
Foreword By
Robby Robinson

Jam' n Java For the Soul
Book One

Written By

Pastor Chuck

Foreword By

Robby Robinson

Featuring Extended Versions of **Pastor Chuck's** Devotionals
Originally Broadcast Worldwide on *Jam' n Java with Robby Robinson*
www.RobbysRecords.com

Jam' n Java Originated as a Ministry of **Trinity Lutheran Church**
Simi Valley, California
www.TrinityLutheranChurchSimi.com

Rev. Robert Lyon Barker, Senior Pastor

Scripture quotations are from the **ESV®** Bible **(The Holy Bible, English Standard Version®),** © 2001 by Crossway, a publishing ministry of Good News Publishers, **ESV®** Text Edition: 2025. The **ESV®** text may not be quoted in any publication made available to the public by a Creative Commons license. The **ESV®** may not be translated in whole or in part into any other language. Used by permission. All rights reserved.

ISBN: 979-8-9999853-0-9

CEDA'S
PUBLISHING HOUSE

Foreword

By Robby Robinson

Pastor Chuck is my dear friend and Brother-in-Christ. He is a man of many talents - a gifted musician, songwriter, preacher, and artisan of beautiful stained glass. But, more than all of that, he is a faithful witness for Christ and a true servant of God.

His devotions have blessed me in countless ways, and through *Jam' n Java* we've had the privilege of sharing them with people all over the world.

They are heartfelt, powerful, and always point us back to the love of Jesus. Now, gathered in this book, they will continue to inspire, encourage, and strengthen countless hearts and lives.

It is my joy to recommend *Jam' n Java For the Soul: Book One* to you. May Pastor Chuck's words draw you closer to the heart of God, just as they have for me.

- Robby Robinson
Jam' n Java Host and Producer
Music Director for Frankie Valli and the Four Seasons

Dedication

Jam' n Java for the Soul: Book One is dedicated to *Him*, from whom all blessings flow, our **Lord, Jesus Christ**. It is *He* who has blessed me with my faith, my loving, patient, and long-suffering wife, **Marseda,** our six children **(Chuck, Jani, Andrew, Becky, Mike and Kristi**), the four greatest grandchildren in the world **(Abby, Amelia, Will and Audrey**) and my church family spread across America. I have been blessed to serve as your Pastor and your Brother-in-Christ.

Soli Deo Gloria,
Pastor Chuck

With Gratitude

Sincere and heartfelt gratitude to my Brother-in-Christ, *Robby Robinson,* for generously granting his kind permission to publish extended versions of these devotionals, which were originally created for his weekly worldwide online broadcast, *Jam' n Java.* Without *Robby Robinson*, there would be no *Jam' n Java For the Soul.* I am forever grateful for the opportunity to be a part of his incredible program.

Learn more about **Robby Robinson** and *Jam' n Java* at **RobbysRecords.com**. **Robby Robinson** is the executive producer and host at the *Jam' n Java* show, music director at **Trinity Lutheran Church** in Simi Valley, California, **#1 Hypeddit®** recording artist, long-time music director and keyboard player at **Frankie Valli and the Four Seasons®**, **Hammond® Organ** aficionado, pianist, orchestra conductor, composer, singer, songwriter, and producer at **Robby's Records.**

Your Brother-in-Christ,
Pastor Chuck

Introduction

By K.P. Lynne

Pastor Chuck is as authentic, *REAL* and down-to-earth as you and me. Refreshingly honest and genuine, *Pastor Chuck* is a "perfectly imperfect" human being, who is as much in need of *Jesus Christ's* mercy, grace and healing as the rest of us.

That knowledge, in and of itself, makes this publication uniquely different. *Pastor Chuck* is not here to preach down to us, lecture us, judge us or condemn us. His sole purpose is to celebrate the unconditional love, mercy and grace of *Jesus Christ* with us, while inspiring us to look deeper within ourselves, as we examine our own relationship with *God*.

When it comes to *Pastor Chuck*, he displays no airs or holier-than-thou attitudes. He is a humble servant of *Jesus Christ*, gently, yet truthfully, explaining *God's* gift of our eternal salvation...which cannot be bought or earned...but was freely given to us at the *Cross*, through our *Baptism,* and by our acceptance of *Jesus Christ* as our *Lord and Savior.*

Pastor Chuck is a master wordsmith, who lovingly and valiantly proclaims witness to our **Christian** faith, courageously and boldly speaking *"His Word"* while imploring us to live our best earthly lives, as modern-day shepherds.

The words inscribed between these hallowed pages were originally broadcast by *Pastor Chuck* over the *Jam'n Java* show featuring *Robby Robinson.* At the request of loyal *"Jammers"*, as *Jam'n Java* fans are affectionately known, *Pastor Chuck* has written extended versions of his podcast devotionals, questions for personal reflection, and provided his own poignant original prayers, to make *"His Word"* more understandable, accessible and relatable in our harried lives of today's modern world.

The original prayers within this book are exquisite, yet simple, direct from *Pastor Chuck's* heart, for the glory and honor of *Jesus Christ,* and the nourishment of your soul. *Pastor Chuck* is not only an exceptional author, but a shining example of our faith. On a personal note, *Pastor Chuck* is one of those extremely rare, once-in-a-lifetime, best friends who has become my chosen family. Enjoy *Jam'n Java For the Soul!*

- K.P. Lynne
#1 Amazon International Best-Selling Author
Award-Winning Singer/Songwriter

Chapter One

January 1

"When the fullness of time had come, God sent forth His Son, born of a woman, born under the law, to redeem those under the law, that we might receive the adoption of sons."
Galatians 4:4-5

If I may, I would like to suggest it would be good to think about that phrase, "the fullness of time." What does it mean to you? If I were to ask you to rephrase it, how would you do that?

Your Safe Space for Personal Reflection

_____

_____

_____

_____

_____

The book of Ecclesiastes tells us, *"For everything there is a reason, and a time for every purpose under heaven."*

- **A time to be born, a time to die**
- **A time to plant, and a time to reap, and so on and so forth**

But I think St. Paul is saying so much more here with the phrase, "In the fullness of time."

- **At the right moment**
- **When everything came together just as God had planned it**
- **When everything was the way, it was supposed to be, and everyone in the right place…**

As I think about that, about God's timing in life, and in the history of the world, I am amazed.

What St. Paul is saying is there is a pivotal point in the history of the world. And at that point everything God had planned came into focus at one specific place and point. The whole history of the world revolves around this point and place in time.

In the fullness of time – at that point – God sent forth His Son. God sent Him into the chaotic and sometimes mundane moments of life and into the history of the world

God's Son was born. But for what purpose?

For redemption.

For adoption.

For your redemption and mine.

For your adoption and mine, so we might become His sons and daughters.

*But the world asks this question: **So, what?***

That is an important question. It is important because we are broken and wounded.

It is important not, only because of what others have done to us, but because of what we have done to ourselves, as well.

It is important because we are sick, and sometimes lonely, or isolated, and at times feel abandoned.

So, what?

So, at the right moment, when everything was ready, at the perfect time and place, God acted and sent us Jesus.

And here is the point: At the right time, God sent His Son for our redemption and adoption.

For thousands of years God's people were asking, **"When, O Lord?"**

At the right time!

You and I ask that same question, *"When O Lord?"*

And the answer is the same: at the right time!

He who brought all things together, in order, for His plan of salvation to spring forth, has not forgotten you.

No matter what your pain or brokenness might say to you.

No matter how life might seem to knock you down and stomp on you.

You know life will do that.

At the right time, in the fullness of time, when we need it the most, God is our help, our security, and our Savior.

Let us not forget what we are told through the prophet Jeremiah: *I know the plans I have for you...plans for welfare and not for evil, to give you a future and a hope!*

Jeremiah 29:11f

In the fullness of time – Immanuel – God is with us! God is with you, through His Son, Jesus Christ.

No matter what the voices of life may tell you. In sickness, *Immanuel! God is with us.*

In times of doubt or uncertainty*, Immanuel! God is with us.*

In relationships that seem to have gone sour, or financial insecurity, or any of the many problems, and difficulties we struggle with daily*, Immanuel! God is with us!*

Things to think about:

You may not presently be at a moment in your life, where everything seems to be "collapsing in" on you, but you probably know that feeling.

How have you dealt with these periods of time in the past?

Your Safe Space for Personal Reflection

_____

_____

_____

_____

_____

_____

Our emotions often lie to us.

There is an old joke: *"They told me to cheer up, things could be worse! So, I cheered up and sure enough, things got worse."*

How difficult is it for you to believe that even in the hard, and difficult, times of your life God is with you and has not abandoned you?

Are you, or have you been (as I have), at a place in your life where it seems like when you pray there is a "barrier over your head" and your prayers are "bouncing back" at you?

This is where our faith comes in.

Genuine faith grabs ahold of the promises of God and will not let go.

In this case, "God, you promised You are with me, and I trust you, because You cannot lie!"

Let's Pray:

Father in Heaven,

Thank you for the days you have given me. May I use them to honor and glorify You in all that I do! You know what lies before me, during this new year. I don't! That's probably a good thing. It is so easy for me to look at the struggles I might have to go through and only see how difficult and impossible they seem.

It's so easy to lean upon my own understanding and strength. And when I do that, I fail! What I do know is that no matter what happens, whether it be for good or ill, my life, my days, my circumstances, are in Your hands.

And that's the best place I can be! In Your hands I am safe and secure, and I know that **"all things work together for good to those who love You and are called according to Your purpose."**

Bless this new year for me according to Your grace and mercy. Help me to trust You in all that I do.

I lift up to you, in prayer, all those who are sick and recovering from illness. I ask that you pour out Your Holy Spirit with extra measure of Your healing grace on them. In Jesus' precious name.

Amen

Chapter Two

January 9

I'd like to share a quote from **Martin Luther** one of my friends posted on Facebook:

"Preach and live as if Jesus was crucified yesterday, rose from the dead today, and is returning tomorrow!"

I really like that because it makes me focus on my life from a different perspective than I normally do. It's one I need to think about.

The quote made me ask myself how different my life would be if I lived that way.

St. Paul says something very close to that in Romans 6 as he writes:

> *Do you not know that all of us who have been baptized into Christ Jesus were baptized into his death? [4] We were buried therefore with him by baptism into death, in order that, just as Christ was raised from the dead by the glory of the Father, we too might walk in newness of life. [5] For if we have been united with him in a death like his, we shall certainly be united with him in a resurrection like his.* (verses 3-5)

So, let's think about your life in connection to your baptism for a couple of moments. If you're like me, you probably don't remember your baptism, because you were baptized as an infant. Those who were baptized as a young person or adults probably do remember their baptism.

That has certain advantages when I think about it. But what is important is that in our baptism we were tied to the death and resurrection of Jesus. So, if we live today as if Jesus was crucified yesterday, we will live as if we died with Him; and all our sins and failings in life died there with Him.

But that was yesterday. And if we remember what Luther said and live as if Jesus was crucified yesterday and rose from the dead today, that brings us an added perspective that is very powerful.

St. Paul says in Romans 6, **"Death no longer has dominion over him…"**That means that through our baptism death no longer has dominion over us. Jesus rose and so shall we! And that frees us up to live as if Jesus is returning tomorrow. Or, as St Paul says in Romans 6:11 "**So you also must consider yourselves dead to sin and alive to God in Christ Jesus.**"

Whatever is going on in your life today is temporary!

Even if you've been told it will be long term. But through our baptism we rise each day as a new person in Christ Jesus. And if we live as if He is returning tomorrow, or maybe the day after, we have the power of baptism that enables us to live victoriously. Even when things are not going well.

In our baptism, we are tied to Jesus who was crucified yesterday. And, in our baptism, we rose from the dead today because that's the power of the Holy Spirit that is at work in us.

Is Jesus coming back tomorrow? None of us knows. But if we live as if He is, through the power of our baptism, we are prepared!

Some things to think about:

All of us have memories of past failures in our lives. We also have certain "weaknesses" that may continually or occasionally plague us.

How helpful is it to know that in Christ Jesus all of that "stuff" has been nailed to the cross with Him and is completely paid for?

Does it give you a sense of freedom knowing all of that "garbage" is "dead and buried" because of Jesus' death and resurrection on your behalf?

It may be helpful to think about it in this way; each of us has many enemies who will bring up our past failures and weaknesses. Even our own conscience will accuse us and try to convince us we are not "worthy" of God's love and forgiveness. The good news is our forgiveness doesn't depend on us, but upon God. Therefore, it is secure!

Your Safe Space for Personal Reflection

_____

_____

_____

_____

_____

Let's Pray:

Father in Heaven,

It is so easy to focus on the problems of today or our current situation and circumstances which, in reality, are only momentary.

Help me to live as a person who has died and has been raised with Christ.

Help me to rediscover the freedom to live above all the things that would drag me down and enslave me.

And help me to live in joyous celebration knowing that nothing can separate me from Your love.

There are problems or difficulties I face but help me to realize that I do not face them alone.

Help me to see Your hand of mercy and grace leading me through these things. There are also people whose situations or circumstances cause me to be concerned on their behalf.

Some of them suffer from terrible disease or illness. Some of them face difficult relationships or financial hardships. Some may have wandered from you.

Father, hear the cries of their hearts. Assure them as You have assured me that You will be with them and answer their concerns according to Your will.

May Your hand of blessing be on me and may I always glorify You as I consider myself dead to sin and alive to You in Christ Jesus. In Jesus' precious and powerful name.

Amen

Chapter Three

Jam'n Java
For the Soul

Book One

January 16

1 Corinthians 1:4-9

I'd like to share a couple of thoughts with you in conjunction with Dr. Martin Luther King, Jr. Day and a portion of 1 Corinthians 1:4-9.

St. Paul writes:

I give thanks to my God always for you because of the grace of God that was given you in Christ Jesus, [5] that in every way you were enriched in him in all speech and all knowledge— [6] even as the testimony about Christ was confirmed among you— [7] so that you are not lacking in any gift, as you wait for the revealing of our Lord Jesus Christ, [8] who will sustain you to the end, guiltless in the day of our Lord Jesus Christ. [9] God is faithful, by whom you were called into the fellowship of his Son, Jesus Christ our Lord.

This is a very interesting statement by the Apostle Paul when you understand that this congregation in Corinth was what probably caused him more headaches than any other congregation in the early church. There was more than one false doctrine being taught.

There were divisions and groups within the fellowship working against each other. There was a specific sexual sin that was tolerated withing the fellowship, and there was also what we might call a "worship problem" as well.

One of the common practices in the early church was the celebration of the Lord's Supper around a fellowship meal. Some of the members would bring a lot of food, but they would also start eating and drinking before others came, especially those who were poor. When they arrived, nothing would be left for them. And these folks who couldn't wait often were already drunk when the others arrived. In other words, as one of my professors from the Sem said, *"It sounds like a 20th century congregation!"*

This congregation in Corinth was filled with all kinds of problems, and yet St Paul could write, "*I give thanks to my God always for you because of the grace of God that was given you in Christ Jesus.*"

Why would he say that to a congregation that was filled with dissention and all kinds of false teaching and practice? Because he recognized *the gift of God's grace that had been given to them in Christ Jesus*.

Many were very poor examples of how a Christian should behave. Some were arrogant and had an attitude of superiority. Some were indifferent to the suffering of their fellow Christians. And some of them elevated what we might call education or intelligence over love and faith.

In spite of all these failures and struggles, St. Paul tells them, "*you are not lacking in any gift, as you wait for the revealing of our Lord Jesus Christ, [8] who will sustain you to the end, guiltless in the day of our Lord Jesus Christ.*"

In other words, no matter their shortcomings, poor witness or their battles with one another, the grace of God would not only sustain them, but present them guiltless on the day when our Lord Jesus returns. Please understand St. Paul isn't saying it doesn't matter what their attitudes toward one another might be, or how they sin against one another.

St. Paul will deal with their problems, sins and inconsistencies throughout this letter. The point is, *THE GIFTS COME FROM GOD AND GOD WILL BRING US TO THE POINT WHERE WE ARE GUILTLESS BEFORE HIM*.

Not because we will be or can be perfect, but because He is perfect, and we have been given His righteousness through our faith which is also His gift to us.

The problem of the church in Corinth was not hatred, or intolerance, or false teaching and practice. Those were the results or symptoms of the problem. The real problem was the condition of sin, just as it is the problem in our country today.

But we would rather talk about the symptoms of the problem, and not the real problem.

I think that's one of the things I appreciate about Dr. King. He made me see I was a part of the problem even if I didn't think I was. That's what the condition of sin does to us; it blinds us to our own failures.

But the Word of God opens our eyes and helps us see, not only our failures, but also the solution: the Grace of God which will sustain us to the end, in spite of our failures and weaknesses.

Our salvation doesn't depend on us and what we might be able to do or not do. It depends on His power to renew and recreate us into His fellowship and body.

It does it through the gift of His grace given to us in our baptism which connects us to the death, resurrection and return of His Son, Jesus Christ.

Some things to think about:

Racism, hatred, intolerance, and bigotry are all the fruit of the sin of refusing to love one another as Jesus has loved us. Are there areas in your life where the fruit of this sin is showing itself?

Jesus' love is a sacrificial love.

That's something all of us struggle with. Are there relationships in your life that have nothing to do with race in which practicing Jesus' love seems impossible?

Your Safe Space for Personal Reflection

_____

_____

_____

_____

Does it free you to hear St. Paul say, "in spite of our failures, God Himself will bring us to the point where we are guiltless before Him"?

That's the point of Jesus' death on our behalf!

Your Safe Space for Personal Reflection

_____

_____

_____

_____

_____

_____

_____

Let's Pray:

Father in heaven, there's an old statement that says if a person isn't a part of the solution, they are a part of the problem. Help us to see our own failures and shortcomings. Help us to see our sins of intolerance and hatred, of indifference and self-centeredness.

Move our hearts to love one another as you have loved us through Your Son, Jesus Christ. Renew and restore us so that we, as brothers and sisters in Christ might glorify You in the way our lives reflect Your love.

Watch over those who put their lives on the line to protect us and keep our nation and our society safe. Guide and direct our leaders and help them to serve You and our nation faithfully. Bless those who lie heavy on our hearts; the sick, hospitalized, and those under the care of health care professionals.

Guide and inspire the doctors and nurses so they might be Your instruments of healing. Help us to love one another Father and be people who reflect Your love and mercy. In Jesus' Name.

Amen

Chapter
Four

February 5

St. Paul wrote to the Corinthians in his first letter, *"I decided to know nothing among you except Jesus Christ and him crucified. And I was with you in weakness and in fear and in much trembling, and my speech and my message were not in plausible words of wisdom, but in demonstration of the Spirit and of power, so that your faith might not rest in the wisdom of men but the power of God."* 1 Corinthians 2:2-5

It's difficult for me to imagine the Apostle Paul as a "man of weakness, fear and trembling" as he describes himself. After all, his letters are so deep and profound and some of the concepts difficult to understand.

And, as we read the book of Acts, we all know that he was no coward. He faced mobs who wanted to kill him, false accusations made before governing officials as well as attempts to assassinate him.

But, by his own words, he describes himself as a man who isn't a great orator or powerful speaker. He says his *"speech and message were not in plausible words of wisdom, but in demonstration of the Spirit and of power."*

What was his message?

"Jesus Christ, and Him crucified!"

That's such a foolish message to the world we live in! It's weak, it has no appeal. But, it is *"the power of God and the wisdom of God!"* (1 Corinthians 1:24)

St. Paul doesn't look on himself as anything special. But look what God did through him! He took a man who was trying to destroy the Church and used him to build and expand it.

He took a man who, by his own account, wasn't very imposing or eloquent, and used him to bring people all over the New Testament world to Christ and to eternal salvation.

What can God do through you? What can He do through me? A lot more than we think He can, because we look at ourselves and see only our weaknesses and limitations.

We hear the voices around us that demean us and point out our failures. But it's not about our strength, ability or wisdom – it's about the power of God. This same power that took a very complex and dedicated man and turned his life around and brought many to know their Savior.

You and I are not called to be another Apostle Paul. We are called to be the man or woman God has redeemed us to be people who know Jesus Christ, and Him crucified!

Some additional thoughts:

One of our military recruitment mottos was, "*Be all that you can be!*"

Often it seems that we live in a world that tells us we can "live up to our potential" but knocks us down when we try to.

How much do the "outside voices" regulate how you feel about yourself?

Take a few moments to do an "inventory" of your gifts, talents and abilities.

Realize that even though there may be many people who have the same combination of gifts that you do, you are still unique, because God created you just the way you are!

What are your strengths?

What are your weaknesses?

What combination of gifts and talents do you have that make you "God's gift to the world?" (Because you really are!)

My God Given Talents and Gifts

_____

_____

_____

_____

_____

How Can I Best Use My Talents and Gifts To Serve God, Myself and Others

_____

_____

_____

_____

_____

Let's Pray:

Father in heaven, forgive our looking at ourselves and seeing only our weaknesses and limitations.

Forgive us for not looking to you to overcome our shortcomings. Help us to see that in every problem we face, every mistake we make, in all our failures the answer is always the same: Christ Jesus and Him crucified.

Pour out Your Holy Spirit and create the fire of faith within us; a faith that looks to You in hope and trust.

Give us a heart filled with thanksgiving because You have made us a unique combination of gifts, talents and abilities. Help us use all of those to serve those around us.

Hear the cries of our hearts as we lift up those who are sick, or lonely, and those wounded by life. Bring healing and comfort to them – and help each of us to be Your instrument of peace. Work in us and work through us to bring life and joy and peace in our world. May we glorify You in all we do. In Jesus' Name.

Amen

Chapter Five

February 13

I suspect you will easily recognize these verses from Matthew 11:28-30.

"Come to me your who labor and are heavy laden, and I will give you rest. Take my yoke upon you, and learn from me, for I am gentle and lowly in heart, and you will find rest for your souls. For my yoke is easy, and my burden is light."

All of us have experienced times or seasons when we just didn't know how we were going to get everything done. In fact, maybe you are in one of those seasons right now.

I don't have as many of those periods of time now as I used to, but I still get them. You know what I mean; too many things to do and not enough time to get it all done. Or times when you have all these demands that have to be met, and people seem to keep adding to the list.

Maybe your first reaction is close to what mine has been a times: you might feel a great deal of anxiety because you just don't know how you're going to get everything done. Or, if you're like me, you might let the frustration build until you get cranky or grumpy. Or maybe you snap at someone because of your frustration or anger.

The only thing that really helps me when I allow this to happen is to do the very thing that Jesus tells us to do in this passage: to stop and take everything to Him.

I find it's often past the time to tell Him what I'm feeling and how I am struggling. It's not that He needs to hear it from me, it's that I need to tell Him in order to recognize it myself.

So often it's not that I have too many things to do, it's that I'm trying to carry all the responsibilities and burdens by myself. It's at those times that I'm not wearing the yoke Jesus would give me. Instead, I have the one I myself have placed on my shoulders.

And those burdens always seem to be more demanding and difficult to carry than the ones Jesus would ask me to carry. I suspect all of us do this and that you know exactly what I'm talking about. And if so, it's no wonder we get tired and weary. It's no wonder we reach a point where it seems we can't go a step farther or don't have enough energy to get it all done.

When I take everything to Jesus, my list of things to do may not have changed. Or perhaps the demands on my time may have become greater than they were before.

But often the anxiety will be gone and I'm able to focus more clearly on what I need to do. I'm also able to set my priorities as well.

Some things to think about:

How comfortable are you with the idea of turning everything that causes you to feel anxious over to Jesus?

_____

_____

_____

This question is more difficult than it seems to answer honestly; Who do you trust more to run your life, you or Jesus?

_____

_____

_____

When you think about the demands on your time what causes you the most anxiety?

Family?

_____

_____

Work?

_____

_____

Social?

_____

_____

Spiritual?

_____

_____

Whether you are feeling anxiety now or suspect you will be soon, let's pray:

Heavenly Father, not everyone is at the place where we feel overwhelmed with the burdens of life and weary with the demands that are placed on us. But all of us have experienced these things from time to time.

For some who are reading this there are so many questions that seem to need answers, and they don't know where to find them. We live under the tyranny of self-imposed demands and high expectation combined with the realization of our failures and weaknesses.

Give us the rest that You have promised us Lord. Take away the burdens that we have placed upon ourselves and replace them with Your yoke. Help us to recognize the difference between what You ask of us and the burdens we place upon ourselves.

Refresh our spirits and renew our strength. Help us to find rest and peace in You through our faith in Your Son, Jesus Christ. Hear the cries of our hearts and the concerns we have for others, Lord. Bring healing to the sick and injured we name before You in our hearts. Comfort those who grieve or mourn. And give to us the peace that passes all understanding. In Jesus' name.

Amen

Chapter
Six

Jam'n Java
For the Soul
Book One

February 20

As I look at the calendar it seems this year is moving by at the speed of light. I can't believe this coming Wednesday is Ash Wednesday. It seems like we just finished singing Christmas Carols and put away the Christmas decorations. The other possibility is it's not that the year is moving faster, but I'm moving a lot slower!

Since Ash Wednesday brings the beginning of the Lenten season, I'd like to take the opportunity to ask you to think about why we celebrate the Lenten season. Advent is about preparing our hearts for the past and future coming of our Savior.

But…what is **Lent** truly all about?

- *Preparation for Easter and Jesus' death and resurrection?*
- *Self-denial?*
- *Observing what it cost God to provide for our salvation?*
- *Probably all of these and more.*

One author I recently read suggested that the Lenten Season, as he put it, is, *"first, last and foremost about baptism!"*

I hadn't thought about it in those terms before, but when I read that, it brought to mind what St. Paul wrote in Romans 6; *"Do you not know that all of us who have been baptized into Christ Jesus were baptized into His death? We were buried therefore with Him by baptism into death, in order that, just as Christ was raised from the dead by the glory of the Father, so we to might walk in newness of life."*

For this author, Lent is about dying and rising with Jesus. Not in some far-off future moment of time, but in the here and now, in the nitty-gritty struggles of everyday life as we experience it. And that speaks directly to me.

Lent is about dying to self so that others might live. It's about dying to all the human ways of thinking and dealing with one another that blind us from seeing the true life that we have with God alone. It's serious because its focus is on Jesus as we watch His battle and victory over every temptation He had to face.

Satan tried to tempt Him to take the world by power, or force, or the showy flash of miracles. Even His own disciples sought to instruct Him in how to "win" as the Messiah.

The Lenten Season reminds us through our faith we have died with Christ, were buried with Him, and rose with Him. So, every day is a new day in which we, by the grace of God, live victoriously over every enemy we face.

Some things to think about:

Which thought do you find more helpful; to think about the Lenten Season in terms of giving something up for God, or, to think about it in terms of what God has given up for you?

_____

_____

_____

Even though you may not remember your baptism, do you find any comfort or strength in knowing that through that baptism you were connected to the death and resurrection of Jesus?

_____

_____

_____

St. Paul points out that through our baptism we are connected to Christ. And being connected to Him means we have His grace and power to "walk in the newness of life."

What does that mean to you in your daily walk with the Lord?

Let's Pray:

Father in Heaven, help us to live in the victory you have given us through our baptism, connected as it is to the death and resurrection of Your Son, Jesus Christ.

That is difficult for us at times as life "happens" around us, and we get lost in concern because of the events, circumstances and situations we experience. But You are the God who brings life out of death and gives us the victory that we cannot gain for ourselves.

Look upon those of us who are going through difficult times and may have questions about the uncertainties of the future. Provide healing for our loved ones and acquaintances who are sick or may be facing surgeries.

Be with the doctors and nurses who minister to them and provide them with guidance, wisdom and insight as they apply their gifts and talents to the needs of their patients.

May Your people glorify You as we walk in our baptismal grace and the "newness of life" You have created for us. In Jesus' name.

Amen

Chapter Seven

Jam'n Java
For the Soul

Book One

February 27

Yesterday was the First Sunday in Lent and the focus of the Scripture lessons was "facing temptation."

In Romans 5, verses 12 and 15, St. Paul writes, ***"just as sin came into the world through one man, and death through sin, and so death spread to all men because all sinned...But the free gift is not like the trespass. For if many died through one man's trespass, much more have the grace of God and the free gift by the grace of that one man Jesus Christ abounded for the many.***"

We don't talk about temptation very much in our society. We may joke about it, as if we can't resist the temptation of having a piece of cake or something like that. We pray in the Lord's prayer, ***"lead us not into temptation..."***. But I'm not sure that we take temptation very seriously.

Until, maybe, we find ourselves struggling with guilt and grief because we are overwhelmed by the consequences of what we have done, have left undone, or because of our failure to resist temptation. Just like Adam and Eve.

There is a kind of parallelism in Scripture, if I can call it that. On the one hand we see the failure of mankind before God. Adam and Eve are the perfect examples for us. But they are not the only ones.

Story after story recounts how all of mankind, even the greatest heroes of the faith, have failed in one way or another.

- *And, as we look at ourselves, we are right there with them!*

On the other hand, there is the example of Jesus. He doesn't fail or fall. He is not overcome by temptation but overcomes not only the temptations, but the Tempter as well. He is victorious.

Whereas you and I have failed before God on one hand along with Adam and Eve, on the other hand we have Jesus who is victorious. We fail and fall. Jesus succeeds and is victorious.

So, what does that mean for us?

- *I like the way my Pastor, Rev. Robert Lyon Barker III said it yesterday in his sermon: "Jesus strapped us to His back and carried us with Him through temptation!"*

That's what St. Paul is saying in Romans 5, *"If many died through one man' trespass, much more has the grace of God and the free gift by the grace of that one man Jesus Christ abounded for many."*

As you and I stand before God, if we try to base our relationship with Him on our own merits and accomplishments, we are failures. We struggle. We fall. We are not the people we are supposed to be.

But, over and over again, we discover we are not on our own because Jesus Christ has "strapped us to His back" and carried us through not only temptation, but through our failures and everything that would separate us from God.

- *He has brought us through it all. God's grace has abounded for the many. The free gift has been given. Not just for the many, but specifically – for you. And for me!*

Some things to think about:

One of the most difficult things in life for us to admit is that we have failed before God. It's easy to rationalize away our sin.

What does St. Paul's teaching about Jesus' death overcoming our trespasses mean to you?

_____

_____

_____

_____

_____

What does the idea that "Jesus strapped us to His back and carried us through temptation" mean to you?

_____

_____

_____

_____

_____

Let's Pray:

Father in heaven, we do fail You. We do falter. We do struggle. We are not the people you call us to be. But, over and over again, we discover our relationship to You is not about what we can or cannot do, or how we have succeeded or failed. It's about what You have done, and continue to do for us through Your Son, Jesus Christ.

Over and over again, our failures become His, because He has taken our failures upon Himself. And His victory becomes ours because He has *"strapped us to His back and carried us through it all"* in our baptism, and as He suffered, died and rose again. Help us to live the victorious life You have created for us.

Reach out with Your grace and mercy and touch those who we know to be sick or injured. Bring them healing. Guide the physicians and nurses that minister to them and grant them wisdom and insight as they use the gifts and talents You have given them.

In all things may we serve and glorify You. In Jesus' name we ask all of this.

Amen

Chapter Eight

Jam'n Java
For the Soul
Book One

March 6

I'd like to share some thoughts with you based on a couple of similar stories in the New Testament.

- *The first is the story of the healing of Jairus' daughter, and the second is the boy with an evil spirit.*

Jairus was a man of some importance, and his daughter was close to dying. So Jairus went to Jesus and asked Him to come, lay His hands of her and heal her.

- *As they were going to the home of Jairus, a man came and told Jairus, "Don't bother the master, your little girl is dead." Jesus told Jairus, "Just believe."*

When they got to Jairus' home, a crowd of mourners had gathered and Jesus asked them why they were mourning and said, *"She is not dead, but only asleep."*

And, of course, the crowd ridiculed Him.

But Jesus commanded the crowd to leave and went into the house with her parents and commanded the little girl to arise.

And she did – full of health.

In the second story, a father brings his son to Jesus to cast out an evil spirit that would seize the boy and throw him into the water or fire trying to kill the lad.

- The father actually said, *"If you can heal him."*
- To which Jesus challenged him and responded, *"If? All things are possible for one who believes."*

I love the father's response here, because I see myself in it. He says to Jesus, *"I believe, help my unbelief!"*

There are probably a lot of times in our lives where we are like both of those fathers; driven by desperation to go to Jesus when something beyond our control is happening.

But do we hear Jesus words, *"Just believe"*? Secondly, do we grab ahold of that command?

The boys' father states very clearly our problem; we believe, but…we still have our doubts. We struggle to believe.

And then there are those who tell us to give up, like the man who told Jairus it was hopeless because his daughter had died. And there are people like the ones who ridiculed Jesus for saying she was asleep and not dead.

I suspect Jairus was what we sometimes call being "shell-shocked." And by that, I mean he was going through the motions. He was struggling to make sense of it all, and it was like he was walking through a bad dream that was all too real.

So, beloved, what are you going through? What problems, what circumstances, what situations, what uncertainties are you facing or trying to work through?

_____

_____

_____

_____

And can you hear Jesus saying to you, "Just believe!"? And if so, what goes through your mind?

_____

_____

_____

_____

I'm sure you have noticed, I am really asking you about your faith.

A lot of people in our country say they believe in Jesus or God. But, the Apostle James tells us, *"even the demons do that, and tremble!"*

To put it simply, faith is nothing less than grabbing ahold of God's promises and not letting go of them, no matter what the world or even our own eyes, intellect or emotions might tell us.

Faith is clinging to God, even when those around us, or our own doubts and uncertainties tell us it is useless. There are those times in life when all of us are like that father who said to Jesus, *"I believe, help my unbelief."*

I know I'm not going to get everything I pray for, and that's probably a good thing. But I do know that no matter what happens to me, no matter what I'm going through, no matter the situation or circumstances of life, my Lord has promised me He will never leave me or forsake me.

And even when things turn out differently than I hoped or desired, I am still in His hands and I am safe. And that's the best place for me to be. Until the next situation comes along, and I have to learn to grab ahold of His promises all over again.

Some things to think about:

If you are not going through a period of uncertainty and doubt at this moment, can you remember a time when you did?

_____

_____

_____

_____

_____

How did you make it through that moment in time? Did you "reach out to Jesus?" Did you "grab a hold" of His promises and not let go?

_____

_____

_____

_____

_____

Let's Pray:

Father in heaven, You know the burdens on every heart.

You know the uncertainties each of us faces. You know the doubts that plague us. You know the difficulties we are going through as well as the sense of loneliness or isolation some feel. You know our insecurities and our fears.

Sometimes, even though we know to whom we should go, we don't. We have difficulty turning things over to you because we struggle with letting go of things.

We really do want to believe, but like the father of the boy who was plagued with an evil spirit, we struggle.

Lord, hear the cries of each heart. Enable us to grab a hold of Your promises and to cling to them no matter what the world around us, or life or even our own eyes tell us.

Help us to put our hope and our trust in You. Bring healing to this fractured world of ours through Your Gospel. And may we be instruments of Your healing peace. In Jesus' name.

Amen

Chapter Nine

March 13

After church yesterday, Robby Robinson made the mistake of telling me I could share any "wisdom" I might have on the Paschal Greeting of Easter.

Robby was referring to the greeting: "He is risen!" And the response: "He is risen indeed! Alleluia!" Let me start with a brief story and then talk a little about this in connection to Luke 24.

Years ago, when I was preparing for my Easter Sunday message I came across this story about a Russian Commissar who was addressing a large gathering of citizens shortly after the Bolsheviks had taken over in Russian.

He lectured them on how the church was a part of the power structure that had kept them in slavery and oppressed them.

The new government, he said, would now lead and direct them because the government would see that everyone was treated fairly. The people didn't need the church because religion was, after all, as Lenin said, "the opiate of the people."

After he finished, he asked if there were any questions or comments.

An old man, dressed in shabby clothing raised his hand and was invited to come to the platform. The old man shuffled his way to the platform, bowed in respect to the commissar, turned to the audience and said, **"He is risen!"** And the audience thundered back, "**He is risen indeed! Alleluia!**"

- *That statement, known as the Paschal Greeting, or the Easter Acclamation, is the bedrock of our faith.*

We don't really know when it was first spoken or began to be used. There is a tradition among some churches that it was first spoken by **Mary Magdalene** when she proclaimed the Gospel to the Emperor Tiberius in Rome. But there is no actual record of that in the Gospels.

There is another tradition which suggests the words **"He is risen!"** were spoken at the **Baptism of St. Augustine** on Easter Eve in 387 AD. It has also come down to us as a part of the **Paschal Homily of St. John Chrysostom**, who was the Archbishop of Constantinople in 386 AD. The first written record of it is around 400 AD.

No matter when this Easter Acclamation began or developed it is, as I mentioned, the bedrock of our doctrine and faith as Christians.

- I can almost see this greeting being used by the disciples themselves in Luke 24 in the story of the disciples traveling to Emmaus on Easter Sunday. If you remember, two disciples were walking to the village of Emmaus and discussing, not only Jesus' death, but also the rumors they had heard that he was alive. A stranger approached them and asked what they were talking about. When they told Him He then explained the Scriptures to them.

The stranger was Jesus, of course, but they didn't recognize Him.

When they reached Emmaus, Jesus was invited to join the disciples and stay overnight with them.

At dinner Jesus took bread, blessed it, broke it, handed it to them, and disappeared.

This was when it dawned on these two disciples they had truly been with *Jesus.*

The two immediately hustled back to Jerusalem to tell the other disciples what they had experienced.

Luke writes in chapter 24:34-36; they found the eleven disciples and those with them who were saying,

- *"The Lord has risen indeed and has appeared to Simon." Then they told what had happened on the road, and how he was known to them in the breaking of the bread. As they were talking about these things, Jesus Himself stood among them and said to them, "Peace be with you."*

I realize the Paschal Greeting isn't actually mentioned in this passage, but I think the general idea of it is there. It stands as a powerful affirmation of our faith, not only in the resurrection of Jesus from the dead, but in the justification that is ours by the grace of God as well as the forgiveness of sins that has been won and given to us through God's grace and mercy.

He has risen, victoriously over sin, death and all the accusations of the law against us, as St Paul puts it. He has risen victoriously over every enemy we face. He has risen over everything that would separate us from Him.

- *There is no situation, no circumstance, and not even our own failures or weaknesses that can keep us from Him.*

As St. Paul says in Romans 8: "**Nothing can separate us from the love of God that is in Christ Jesus, our Lord.**"

Some things to think about:

I find that in my own life it has been difficult for me to "let go" and turn to God when problems "come a calling."

A part of that is the influence of our society that stresses self-sufficiency. Another part of that is our pride that doesn't want God's influence or control in our lives.

How quickly are you able to turn things over to God in a difficult situation? Have you reached that point in your life?

_____

_____

_____

_____

_____

_____

Let's Pray:

Father in heaven, You know the heartaches and burdens each one of us is carrying. You know that in so many ways we are tired and weary, weak, heavy laden, isolated, confused, restless and afraid.

Lord, take all of these burdens from us. Heal our heartaches and dry our tears. Wrap Your arms around us and daily lead us through our faith and give us the confidence that You will never abandon or forsake us.

Hear also the cries on our hearts for others. Father, provide healing for all of those we name before You in our own hearts. Bless the ministries of the doctors and nurses that minister to those we love and grant them extra measure of wisdom and insight.

Use us to proclaim Your promises in our thoughts, words and deeds. May we glorify You in all that we do. In Jesus' name we pray.

Amen

Beloved, **HE IS RISEN! HE IS RISEN INDEED! ALLELUIA!**

Chapter
Ten

Jam'n Java
For the Soul

Book One

March 20

As I write this we are into the fourth week of Lent and Easter is only 20 days away. The days seem to be flying by.

I'd like to share one of the readings for our worship service yesterday as a part of the lessons for the fourth Sunday in Lent, Ephesians 5:8-14.

St. Paul writes:

At one time you were in darkness, but now you are light in the Lord. Walk as children of light (for the fruit of light is found in all that is good and right and true) and try to discern what is pleasing to the Lord. Take no part in the unfruitful works of darkness but instead expose them. For it is shameful even to speak of the things they do in secret. But when anything is exposed by the light, it becomes visible for anything that becomes visible is light. Therefore, it says, 'Awake O Sleeper, and arise from the dead, and Christ will shine on you."

One of the things which struck me yesterday when I heard this passage read was that this is what the season of Lent is all about, trying to take the time to reflect on our personal relationship with our God.

And in that reflection, to let the light of God shine on the dark places in our lives. The purpose of this is that as these dark areas are exposed, we can change our lives by walking as children of Light and trying to discern what is pleasing to God.

- ***There are a lot of wonderful things in this life.***

However, it is easy to become distracted and forget our calling to walk as children of light. In examination of my own life, I can see areas when my walk is not what it should be.

There are areas that need to be changed. It is a lot easier said than done. I don't like the areas of darkness in my life being exposed. It's painful to give some of those things up. But I've also discovered that it's not as painful as hanging on to them!

- ***Before us is the cross of Jesus. And that cross reminds us of what God said about all of this through Jesus own words: "It is finished!"***

Those are not words of condemnation or judgment against us. They are words of mercy and grace. ***What is "finished" is our separation from God.***

And it is finished because Jesus has taken upon Himself the burden of our debt. Through His death and resurrection, Jesus' blood has redeemed and reclaimed us. We belong to Him and have claimed the new life that is in Him through our faith. So, let us walk as those who belong to Him, as those who belong to the Light.

Some things to think about:

If you are honest with yourself and God, what are the dark areas of your life?

It may be helpful to confess those dark areas to someone you can trust and is a mature Christian. Make sure it is someone who will not judge you but will speak the words of forgiveness and restoration as well.

Every Christian fails.

Not a single one of us can stand before God on our own merits. It is only through Jesus that we can find comfort and strength in the words, *"It is finished!"*

It might not seem like the dark areas of your life are "**finished.**"

But the **victory** is ours, even though the *"war"* still goes on inside us.

Let's Pray:

Father in heaven, send Your Holy Spirit to us and help us to use this Lenten season not only to examine our own life but also to help us walk as children of light.

Help us also to study the love and mercy which You have made visible to us in the suffering and death of Your Son, our Lord Jesus Christ.

Help us to discern what is pleasing to You. Fill our hearts with the peace that surpasses all understanding. Give us the trust and confidence to know that You have heard the cries of our hearts.

You know the concerns and difficulties of life that can weigh us down. You know where each of us struggles, and You know our own personal fears and our lack of understanding. Speak to our hearts and bring us peace.

May we glorify You as we celebrate the light and life You have given us in Jesus our Savior. It's in His name that we pray.

Amen

Chapter Eleven

Jam'nJava
For the Soul
Book One

March 27

I'd like to share a couple of thoughts with you based on Matthew 11:28-29:

Jesus said, "***Come to me all of you who labor and are heavy laden, and I will give your rest. Take my yoke upon you and learn from me, for I am gentle and lowly in heart, and you will find rest for your souls.***"

There are times in my life I have wanted to share how great and wonderful the love and mercy of God is with others. I have wanted to share how He has touched my life with his profound compassion and mercy. I've yearned to preach the one special sermon that somehow flips the switch in someone's mind and leads them directly to God.

I've longed to write the one Christian song that touches the hearts of all who hear it and convinces them to follow Jesus. I've wanted to do something with stained glass which would serve as a permanent testimony and ongoing witness to my Lord and Savior.

The goal would not be for myself to be praised or remembered, but for our God of creation, God of our salvation, and God of redemption to be honored and glorified though my creative works.

But there's a problem: nothing is ever good enough.

Everything falls short when compared to His majesty and glory. There's always a flaw: a phrase that could be expressed more clearly or a piece of glass that breaks during installation.

I shared that with a friend recently and he said, "Well, that's appropriate. After all, we're all broken too!"

And indeed, we are. We come to God broken and incomplete, filled with inadequacies and failures, overloaded with guilt and weighed down with shame.

And what is God's response to us? He puts the broken pieces back together and makes our weaknesses perfect through His strength. He fills our empty hearts with His love and washes away our sin as He wraps His arms around us.

The season of Lent will always point out our inadequacies and failures. Not in order that we might be brought low or humiliated, but that Jesus might be honored and, above all, trusted by placing our faith in Him. The Lenten Season is about helping us to see God's open arms and the forgiveness that is ours in Christ Jesus.

Some things to think about:

Some people point out our failures and inconsistencies to dominate or control us. The Law of God points out our failures to show us the complete and full love of God. ***God's intent is not to "bring us low" but to "lift us up" and free us from the burden of guilt.*** Have you ever felt that nothing is ever good enough in your life? Whether it's a criticism from others or a self-evaluation from within you, here's the bad news: it's accurate (if perfection is the goal). ***Here's the good news: It doesn't matter because Jesus can use it no matter how inadequate you or others might think it is.***

Let's Pray:

Father in Heaven, no matter how inadequate our words or thoughts might be, we still offer You our worship and praise. Be glorified by the cries of our hearts that would offer to You all glory and honor. In Your love for us You sent Your son Jesus to be our Savior and Redeemer. You have claimed us as Your own and made us into Your family. May we in service to You and love for one another glorify You in all that we do. Hear the petitions we would place before You on behalf of those for whom we are concerned. Might they, and we, find healing, rest and peace in You. In Jesus name we pray. Amen.

Chapter Twelve

Jam'n Java
For the Soul

Book One

April 3

We are in Holy Week now and I'd like to take a few moments to explain some very significant things many **Christians do not understand about Holy Week in this day and age.**

On Palm Sunday, Jesus entered into Jerusalem. On Thursday Jesus and His disciples will celebrate the Passover. But, on Sunday, He makes it clear to every Jew observing that He is the promised Messiah. How? By riding into Jerusalem on a donkey. This was foretold by the prophet.

Then he went to the temple and cleansed it by casting out the money changers and the merchants. He would spend the rest of the week teaching.

On Thursday he directed two of His disciples to go to a certain home where there was a large upper room, and to prepare for their celebration of the Passover.

This was a bit unusual because the Passover celebration would begin at sundown on Friday evening. **But Jesus would be on the cross and dead by sundown on Friday.** That's one point we often miss.

Remember that ***John the Baptizer*** had called Jesus, ***"The Lamb of God that takes away the sin of the world."*** And indeed, He was.

As Jesus and His disciples gathered for the Passover celebration that Thursday evening, the disciples were engaged in one of their usual activities, arguing over which of them was the greatest, and who would get the positions of honor.

Jesus puts a stop to all this nonsense by telling them, ***"A new commandment, I give unto you, that you love one another even as I have loved you."***

He then proceeded to give them a ***powerful object lesson.***

One of the traditions of the day was when people had a gathering, a member of the household would welcome the attendees by washing their feet.

This was usually assigned to the person who was the lowest in the household. Or perhaps a slave.

But men who are arguing about who's the greatest don't lower themselves to this humiliating and humbling task. So, Jesus Himself took off His outer robes, wrapped a towel around Himself and washed their feet.

Jesus then told them, and I'm paraphrasing here, *"You call me Master and Lord, and it is right for you to do so. So, if I can treat you this way, this is the way you are to treat one another."*

This is where we get the name, "**Maundy Thursday**" Maundy comes from the Latin, "Mandate" which means, "command."

- *Jesus has given His disciples a new commandment: to love one another as He has loved us.*

During the Passover meal itself, Jesus then took some unleavened bread, blessed it, and broke it and gave it to the disciples.

- *Jesus gave them these words, "Take, and eat. This is my body given for you for you for the forgiveness of sins. Do this in remembrance of me."*

- Then, a little later, Jesus took one of the cups of wine and told them, *"This is my blood of the new covenant, shed for you for the forgiveness of sins. Drink of it, all of you. Do this in remembrance of me."*

At the conclusion of the meal, they left the upper room and went to the *Garden of Gethsemane.*

This is where Jesus would spend the next few hours in prayerful preparation for the ordeal which lay ahead of Him. He would be arrested, put through at least three phony and illegal trials, beaten, scourged, humiliated, and crucified.

During His crucifixion darkness would cover the land for three hours as He suffered for the sins of the world.

At the end, He would say, *"It is finished!"* and surrender His Spirit into His Father's hands.

- *An earthquake would shake the area and the curtain in the Temple which separated the Holy of Holies from the sanctuary would be torn from top to bottom signifying that the perfect sacrifice, the Lamb of God, was complete and Jesus had made the perfect Atonement for the sins of the world.*

One of the things that I think we should think about is that none of this is by accident. It is all what we might call the "Divine Drama" played out in this world for one purpose: the salvation of man.

One other important thing: It is Jesus who is in control, not His enemies. He knew who He was and what His mission was. He was the only One who could accomplish our Salvation. And He did it even at the cost of His life.

Some things to think about:

Have you ever thought about your life as being a part of "the Divine Drama" of God's plan of salvation?

Safe Space for Your Thoughts

The "Divine Drama" didn't end with the resurrection and ascension of Jesus into heaven. It is still being played out in the lives of His people. Your life isn't a waste! You aren't "useless" and you haven't been or won't be abandoned.

As a person who believes in Jesus Christ as your Savior, your God is doing great things through you even though you may not see it.

Let's Pray:

Father in heaven, during this Holy Week celebration, draw us closer to You as we view once again all that You have done for us through our Savior, Jesus Christ.

Jesus is the very Lamb of God who takes away the sin of the world including our sin as well.

Give us not only a deeper understanding of the cost of our salvation but create a deeper faith within us that trusts You implicitly no matter the struggles or difficulties we might be going through today or in the future.

Be present with those who are going through difficult times, whether they are going through some of the problems of life, or illness or just the stuff that seems to happen to us.

Father give all of us peace that surpasses all understanding so we might know we are safe and secure in Your loving hands. In all that we do may we glorify You. In Jesus' name.

Amen

Chapter Twelve

Jam'n Java
For the Soul
Book One

April 10

Let's Begin Here:

HE IS RISEN!

HE IS RISEN INDEED!

ALLELUIA!

The evangelist Luke continues the Easter story for us in this way: Luke 24:13-35;

13 Now that same day two of them were going to a village called Emmaus, about seven miles from Jerusalem. 14 They were talking with each other about everything that had happened. 15 As they talked and discussed these things with each other, Jesus himself came up and walked along with them; 16 but they were kept from recognizing him.

17 He asked them, "What are you discussing together as you walk along?"
They stood still, their faces downcast. 18 One of them, named Cleopas, asked him, "Are you the only one visiting Jerusalem who does not know the things that have happened there in these days?"

19 "What things?" he asked.

"About Jesus of Nazareth," they replied. "He was a prophet, powerful in word and deed before God and all the people. [20] The chief priests and our rulers handed him over to be sentenced to death, and they crucified him; [21] but we had hoped that he was the one who was going to redeem Israel. And what is more, it is the third day since all this took place. [22] In addition, some of our women amazed us. They went to the tomb early this morning [23] but didn't find his body. They came and told us that they had seen a vision of angels, who said he was alive. [24] Then some of our companions went to the tomb and found it just as the women had said, but they did not see Jesus."

[25] He said to them, "How foolish you are, and how slow to believe all that the prophets have spoken! [26] Did not the Messiah have to suffer these things and then enter his glory?" [27] And beginning with Moses and all the Prophets, he explained to them what was said in all the Scriptures concerning himself.

[28] As they approached the village to which they were going, Jesus continued on as if he were going farther.

29 But they urged him strongly, "Stay with us, for it is nearly evening; the day is almost over." So he went in to stay with them.30 When he was at the table with them, he took bread, gave thanks, broke it and began to give it to them. 31 Then their eyes were opened and they recognized him, and he disappeared from their sight. 32 They asked each other, "Were not our hearts burning within us while he talked with us on the road and opened the Scriptures to us?"

33 They got up and returned at once to Jerusalem. There they found the Eleven and those with them, assembled together 34 and saying, "It is true! The Lord has risen and has appeared to Simon." 35 Then the two told what had happened on the way, and how Jesus was recognized by them when he broke the bread.

So let me ask you to think about the road you're walking today. Maybe the path you have been on has led you through some difficult times or made you go through some uncertainty.

Maybe you have experienced a painful loss or received a doctor's diagnosis that confirmed your worst fears.

There have been times when I have felt as if the road I was on was not only filled with pain, but loneliness as well. I felt as if I was facing the most difficult things I've ever had to go through all by myself.

- *Whatever you might be going through, you are not alone.*

I imagine the two disciples headed for Emmaus were filled not only with uncertainty and doubt, but also grief. I assume they were asking themselves what they were supposed to do now – now that it seemed everything about their lives lay in ashes around them. But they were not alone – Jesus was with them.

- *And you and I may never understand why some things happen to us. We may never see a purpose or a reason for these things. But we can be certain of this: we are not alone, and our God will not abandon us to our fears, doubts or uncertainties!*

We are not forgotten, because Jesus, the One crucified for our sins and raised for our justification, walks with us.

As the Apostle Paul reminds us in Romans 8: *"Nothing can separate us from the love of God that is our in Christ Jesus our Lord."*

Some things to think about:

Someone once observed that there is a kind of continuous cycle to life: either we are in the midst of something difficult, have just come out of something difficult, or are about to enter into something difficult. Where are you in this cycle?

Safe Space for Your Thoughts

_____

_____

_____

_____

_____

I'll ask the question again; What kind of road are you on? No matter what kind of road you are on, or what the path might be leading you through, you are not alone. After all, if God offered up His Son on your behalf, He values you and it doesn't make sense for Him to "toss you on the garbage pile" of life!

Let's Pray:

Heavenly Father, it took a bit of time for the two Emmaus disciples to recognize the presence of Your Son as He walked with them.

We are like them. We focus on the difficulties and struggles we are going through and try to reason them out on our own.

So many things are beyond our own understanding.

Help us to focus on Your Word of promise and Your love and mercy. Even though we may not always "feel" Your presence in our lives, help us to experience Your grace and power through Your Word of promise.

Hear the concerns of our hearts. Reassure us and calm our doubts and remove our fears. Give us the confidence of faith and the assurance that we are never alone, for You walk with us. May we glorify You in all that we do. In Jesus name.

Amen

Chapter Thirteen

Jam'n Java
For the Soul
Book One

April 17

I'd like to share a couple of thoughts tonight on one of Jesus' disciples who is often given a bad reputation: Thomas, called "The Twin", among the disciples. The one often called, "Doubting Thomas."

Thomas is mentioned in the New Testament only eight times and four of those times are when Jesus' disciples are listed.

Most of what we know about him is given to us in the Gospel of John. In John 20 we are told that he refused to accept the testimony of his fellow disciples that Jesus had risen.

And that is the reason he is given the nickname of *"Doubting Thomas."*

But in John 11, when the disciples are trying to discourage Jesus from going to Jerusalem because it's too dangerous and He might get arrested, it is Thomas who says, *"Let us go with Him, that we may die with Him."*

In John 14, when Jesus is trying to prepare His disciples for the events that lay ahead, He says, **"Let not your hearts be troubled. Believe in God, believe also in me.[2] In my Father's**

House are many rooms. If it were not so, would I have told you that I go to prepare a place for you ³ *And if I go and prepare a place for you, I will come again and will take you to myself, that where I am you may be also.* ⁴ *And you know the way to where I am going."*

It is Thomas who asks, *"Lord, we do not know where you are going. How can we know the way?"* And that's the place where Jesus says those words that give us so much comfort, *"I am the way, the truth and the life. No one comes to the Father except through me."*

Here's one other thought we often forget: Thomas wasn't the only disciple who had doubts about Jesus' resurrection.

Luke tells us, *"When they* (the women) *came back from the tomb, they told all these things to the Eleven and to all the others. It was Mary Magdalene, Joanna, Mary the mother of James, and the others with them that told this to the apostles. But they did not believe the women, because their words seemed to them like nonsense."*

Was it just because they were women that the Eleven didn't believe? Or was it because they, just like Thomas, were filled with doubt and sorrow? I've read comments about this being the result of male chauvinism. But the fact that the disciples were filled with doubt seems much more reasonable.

Here's the point I want to make…all of us have times or periods in life when we question things… where doubts plague us.

In my life those times always seem to happen when major things are taking place such as an illness. Some of you might be facing something like that right now. Or maybe your financial security is in question. Perhaps there seems to be so much stress that life has been turned upside down and you may wonder *where is God in all of this?*

To have doubts and to struggle with uncertainty is not a sin. It does not make you a weak Christian. It only proves you are human.

And being a follower of Jesus is not about how strong or competent you are as a human being.

It is about the grace and mercy of God that is available to you no matter what situation or circumstance you find yourself in. And the best way to handle doubt is to tell the Lord about it.

Some things to think about:

Are you **"holding out on God?"** Are you trying to handle everything on your own? Are there areas of your life that you consider "too minor" or "too unimportant" to bother God with? Here's an important **"news flash"** there is no such thing as a "Super Christian" who is never bothered by uncertainty or plagued with doubt. There are only believers who have been broken by their sin and see the reality of their flaws before God. There are only people who need to come to Him for healing.

So, let's do that! Would you pray with me now?

Father in Heaven,

You are well aware of how we struggle with uncertainty and doubt in our lives. You know the things that are heavy on every heart. Help us to focus this evening not on the questions that are going through our minds, but Your promise that You will never leave us or forsake us.

May Your promise that You are with us, even to the end of the age, comfort and strengthen us. May Your victory over sin and death through the resurrection of Your Son, Jesus, strengthen our faith. And may we recognize, even with our current struggles, all these things work together for our good. And may we glorify You in all that we do. We ask this in Jesus' name.

Amen

Chapter Fourteen

Jam'n Java
For the Soul
Book One

May 1

Yesterday was "*Good Shepherd Sunday*" in our denomination. One of the lessons was the Psalm so many of us know and use as a source of comfort and strength in difficult times; **The 23rd Psalm.**

Let me share it with you now:

The Lord is my shepherd; I shall not want.
2 He maketh me to lie down in green pastures: he leadeth me beside the still waters.
3 He restoreth my soul: he leadeth me in the paths of righteousness for his name's sake.
4 Yea, though I walk through the valley of the shadow of death, I will fear no evil: for thou art with me; thy rod and thy staff they comfort me.
5 Thou preparest a table before me in the presence of mine enemies: thou anointest my head with oil; my cup runneth over.
6 Surely goodness and mercy shall follow me all the days of my life: and I will dwell in the house of the Lord forever.

The 23rd Psalm has always been a comfort to people at the darkest times of life. Why? For one thing, it is beautifully written. And for another thing this life is filled with times of insecurity and doubt for all of us.

We have all walked *"through the valley of the shadow of death"* at times. Maybe because of a very serious surgery we were facing. Maybe we have been in an accident which could have caused our death or the death of a loved one.

- *A monk once put it this way: in the midst of life, death.*
- *But it is also true: in the midst of death: life.*
- *In the midst of death, life because we are being led by the Good Shepherd. In the midst of death life because He is the One who has laid down His life for us. He is the One who calls us by name. He is the One who has prepared and supplied us with all that we need.*

Even when it seems like we are surrounded by enemies, we cannot overcome, He protects and guards us.

He is the One who restores our souls and lifts the burdens from our shoulders.

He is the One who gives us strength and courage to face the days and nights of difficulty.

- *That's why we can say, Even in death: life. Because we belong to Him who is the Good Shepherd.*

Some things to think about:

It's probably easier to recognize the idea of *"in the midst of life: death"* because we know, even though we try to ignore it, we are all going to die. So, death often comes *"in the midst of life."*

How does "in the midst of death: life" change how you can look at life every day?

_____

_____

_____

_____

How does knowing that the Good Shepherd is with you at all times – good and bad – help you as you walk the path you are on today?

_____

_____

_____

_____

Let's Pray:

Father in Heaven,

We thank You for the multitude of blessings You have poured out upon us.

Even as we face uncertain days, uncertain health, or any of life's current or forthcoming problems, we are safe and secure because we belong to You and we are Yours.

Grant each of us the faith to understand no matter what problems we might be facing, and no matter what our struggles might be, we are not alone.

You are not only with us, but You are leading us through these times and You will guide us safely through them.

Hear the cries of our hearts, O Lord. Help us to place our trust in Your love and Your mercy, for only You know what is best for each one of us.

Thank You for Your faithfulness and goodness to us. And may our own personal lives reflect Your love and glorify Your name. In Jesus' name.

Amen

Chapter Fifteen

JaM'n Java
For the Soul

Book One

May 22

I would like to focus on a few verses from Psalm 68.

David writes:

> *God shall arise, his enemies shall be scattered; and those who hate him shall flee before him!*

> *As smoke is driven away, so you shall drive them away, so you shall drive them away; as wax melts before fire, so the wicked shall perish before God.*

> *But the righteous shall be glad; They shall exult before God. They shall be jubilant with joy!*

> *Sing to God, sing praises to his name; lift up a song to him who rides through the deserts; His name is the Lord; exult before him!*

While I sometimes may have concerns about my health, my family, and other issues in my own life, I haven't been filled with extreme uncertainty and fear. **Why?** Not because I have such a great and powerful faith. But because I know that no matter what may happen, our God is always in control. Also, as Paul says in Romans 8, *"all things work together for good to those who love God and are called according to His purpose."*

As I think about my life, I have such a limited perspective.

When I try to look "down the road," as they say, I can't see things very far beyond my own needs and desires.

There may be some outcomes or goals I'd like to reach, but nothing is guaranteed. Sometimes I'm able to reach to a goal I've set, but it's often by a different route than I planned.

- *It's when I look back over my life and the people God has placed in my life that I see how truly blessed I am.*

The friendships and associations that have developed through my relationship to my Lord have truly helped me to grow in His grace. More importantly, I also see how He has overcome every enemy I have had to face and given me the victory.

- *God has done the same for you.*

Your enemies, whether they be health issues, relational difficulties, whatever struggle or situation you have found yourself in, your enemies are God's enemies. And if He hasn't already scattered them, He soon will.

As the psalmist David says, **God shall arise, his enemies shall be scattered; and those who hate him shall flee before him!**

Some things to think about:

Does the idea that your enemies are God's enemies seem impossible to you?

- *Sometimes the struggles of life and their outcomes (such as diminished health) seems to indicate God hasn't scattered our enemies.*
- *Sometimes it seems that His enemies seem to flourish and prosper more than the ones who love Him. Please read Psalm 68 again and grab a hold of the promises God gives you in these verses.*

Let's Pray:

Father in Heaven,

It is so easy to let the concerns of this life cloud our vision and turn our focus inwardly. It is easy to question the events of life and to complain because life doesn't seem fair at times.

Help us to see where You have fought for us and given us the victory.

No matter where we find ourselves in life, help us to believe the wonderful promises Your Word gives us; that You will never abandon us, that You will be with us always, that we need not fear the world or this life because You have already overcome them.

All of us have concerns not only for ourselves but for those we love as well.

And as we come before You in this moment, hear those concerns and help us to trust in Your grace and mercy. Through Your Son, Jesus Christ You have made each of us who believe in Him righteous in Your sight.

And Your servant David assures us tonight that, *the righteous shall be glad; They shall exult before God; They shall be jubilant with joy!*

Help us to sing songs of joy as we celebrate all that You've done for us and will continue to do for us.

We love you, Father. Through our Savior Jesus Christ.

Amen

Chapter Sixteen

Jam'n Java
For the Soul

Book One

May 29

Yesterday was *Pentecost,* the day the church celebrates the outpouring of the *Holy Spirit.* ***In the Church calendar Pentecost is 50 days, or seven weeks after Easter.***

Pentecost coincides with the Jewish celebration, the festival of weeks, which was a harvest festival celebrated seven weeks and one day (50 days) after the first day of Passover. It was one of the three great feasts or celebrations of the Jews. The other two were Passover and the festival of booths, also known as the festival of tabernacles.

These three festivals were the high point of worship and celebration for the Jewish faith. And the goal of most Jews was to celebrate one of these three feasts in Jerusalem at least once in their lives. Particularly Passover. If you lived somewhat close to Jerusalem, it wasn't that difficult. But by the time of Jesus, the Jews lived all over the Roman Empire, so a trip to Jerusalem was a daunting task.

This is why the evangelist Luke lists so many different languages spoken by the Disciples on the day of Pentecost. People from all over the Mediterranean world were in Jerusalem to attend the celebration of the festival of weeks.

This just points out how our God is a master strategist: He uses His resources wisely!

There is something else about this event I think we often miss or don't think about. It's the change in the disciples after the Holy Spirit was poured out on them during Pentecost.

Remember, these were the guys who deserted Jesus in the Garden. Many of them were filled with uncertainty even after they personally saw Jesus after His resurrection. *But when Pentecost happens, the Holy Spirit empowers them, and they are changed.* They are no longer afraid or timid. They begin to preach and teach with power and conviction.

There is one other thing I think we need to remember: these men and women were not suddenly changed into some kind of "super disciples". They still had their times of uncertainty and weakness.

For example, Paul had to correct Peter over the way he was treating the Gentile believers in Galatia. The New Testament church had its controversies and doctrinal struggles. But through all of that, the message of salvation was being proclaimed by common, ordinary folk like you and me.

Let me say it another way: Scripture teaches us when the Holy Spirit works in us, we are God's New creation. For some of us that happens when we come to faith as an adult. For others of us, it happens in the waters of Baptism, even as an infant. And I know this is something denominations disagree on but here's the point of what I think Pentecost is all about.

- *You and I, as believers, have the same gift of the Holy Spirit the Apostles and all those gathered in the upper room were given. We don't have a lessor or inferior amount. We have the same gift, with the same blessings, and the same benefits as did the disciples.*

What are those gifts?

Primarily, the same saving faith and new relationship to God, through our Savior, Jesus Christ.

What is different is the way His gifts are manifested in each of us. Remember the promises Jesus gave to His disciples, living then and today, saying He would not leave us comfortless, but would send the Holy Spirit to us. He also promised that He would never leave us or abandon us.

And as the Apostle Paul reminds us in Romans, the Holy Spirit groans up to God, on our behalf, communicating our needs. Each one of us has been given the same gift of the Holy Spirit, with the same blessings and the same benefits.

- *The expression of these gifts is different in all of us, but the point is this: You have everything you need, no matter where your journey is taking you today or tomorrow, because God has kept His promise. And He will continue to do so.*

It seems impossible for the disciples to be "common folk" just like you and me. In a way they weren't, because they had spent three years under Jesus' instruction. But in other ways they were.

Some things to think about:

So, what are the ways in which you are like the disciples? Is there one particular disciple you identify with most closely? What were his weaknesses? What were his strengths? What do you have in common with him?

Let's Pray:

Father in heaven, thank you for never abandoning us. Thank you for sending not only your Son to be our Savior, but also the Holy Spirit to lead us into faith and to make us your own family.

We thank You Father for those who, out of love for this nation, have willingly walked and run into danger in order to protect and defend this nation.

May we not abuse the privileges and blessings they have given us by apathy and indifference. May we daily recognize the blessings You have poured out upon this nation, and may we live lives that honor You in all that we do.

You know the things that are heavy on each heart this evening. Hear our prayers and petitions on behalf of those we love.

Assure us with the gift of Your peace that our lives are in Your hands and we are safe, no matter what concerns we might have or difficulties we might be going through.

Again, may we glorify You in all that we do. In Jesus name.

Amen

Chapter
Seventeen

Jam'n Java
For the Soul

Book One

June 5

Yesterday was *Trinity Sunday* and the Gospel lesson was Matthew 28:16-20. It's commonly known as the *Great Commission.* This is where Jesus gives the church it's marching orders: we are to go and make disciples.

There are a couple of things we miss in this lesson.

- *Matthew tells us when the eleven met Jesus at a place he had designated, they worshiped Him. That seems proper enough! After all, they had spent three years with Him, had seen all the miracles He had performed, and then had seen Him crucified, dead, buried and resurrected.*

- *But, Matthew adds, some doubted. What? After all of that...some still doubted?*

They met Jesus at this place and worshipped Him, and some still doubted? Yup! I think we sometimes put these men on a high pedestal and forget they were just as human and broken as you and I are. The doubt wasn't the kind that is skepticism or denial.

It wasn't the kind of doubt that refuses to believe. It's the kind of doubt you and I have which sometimes really plagues us.

- **It's the kind of doubt that that we have when we're uncertain over the future. It's the kind of doubt we have when we wonder what the situations and circumstances of our life mean. It's the kind of doubt that is a hesitancy or uncertainty over the experiences of life, and how they are to be understood.**

And that's exactly where you and I find ourselves at times in our lives. Maybe we're trying to understand how our faith and relationship to God fit together when we're struggling with health issues, or financial difficulties, or broken relationships.

- **If that's where you are at this moment, it's okay!**

It's natural. Everyone goes through this stuff. And while we struggle, or face uncertainty; while we have questions and don't know how all of this is going to tie together in life, we have something to focus on that helps us bring it all into perspective.

Jesus said two things to His disciples throughout the ages, (and that includes you and me):

- *First He said, "All authority has been given to me."*
- *Secondly He added, "And, I am with you always, even to the end of the age."*

When we are going though difficulties and struggles; when we don't even know what first step to take, Jesus not only has authority over those difficulties and struggles, but He is also with us from beginning to end as we go through them. That's the promise He has made to us. Whatever you might be going through at this moment – Our Lord Jesus has all authority over it, and He is walking with you through it all.

Some things to think about:

During the difficult times of life, does the concept of Jesus' authority over all things come into your thinking? Why or why not?

_____

_____

_____

In this world there are those who may have great authority, but also have little concern, compassion or desire to use it for the benefit of others. How is Jesus different?

_____

_____

_____

_____

How would focusing on Jesus' authority and presence in your life instead of the current situation or circumstances make your walk different?

_____

_____

_____

_____

_____

Let's Pray:

Father in heaven, help us to take all of the things that trouble us, all of the uncertainties and difficulties of life and to lay them at the foot of the cross where they belong.

Help us to focus not on the difficulties or the struggles we face, but the promises of Your power and presence even when things seem bleak.

Help us to remember that nothing can separate us from Your love through Christ Jesus our Lord.

Help us to celebrate all that You have done and continue to do for us in this life.

May our lives glorify You no matter what the circumstances or situations of life we find ourselves in might be. In Jesus' name.

Amen

Chapter Eighteen

Jam'n Java
For the Soul
Book One

June 19

I'd like to share a portion of Romans 5:6-11.

St. Paul writes:

> *For while we were still weak, at the right time Christ died for the ungodly. [7]*
> *For one will scarcely die for a righteous person—though perhaps for a good person one would dare even to die - [8] but God shows his love for us in that while we were still sinners, Christ died for us. [9]*
> *Since, therefore, we have now been justified by his blood, much more shall we be saved by him from the wrath of God. [10]*
> *For if while we were enemies we were reconciled to God by the death of his Son, much more, now that we are reconciled, shall we be saved by his life. [11] More than that, we also rejoice in God through our Lord Jesus Christ, through whom we have now received reconciliation.*

If you have followed *Jam' n Java* for any time you've heard Robby Robinson talk more than once about the Grace of God using this acronym: God's Riches at Christ's Expense. That's a good place to start as we think about what God has done for us. *But why do we need this grace?*

In the five verses we just read St. Paul uses three phrases to describe every one of us.

We may not like them, but they are accurate and instructive if we hear them properly.

- St. Paul says, *"While we were still weak, While we were still sinners,"* and *"while we were enemies..."*

I imagine that if I told you that you are spiritually weak, a sinner and God's enemy, you wouldn't like it. There's something about these accusations that really grates against the way we think about ourselves.

Especially here in America. We are the people who can get the job done. We're told that there's nothing that can stop us from accomplishing our goals if we set our mind to them. It's ingrained in our culture.

So, it's offensive to us to hear that we are weak, sinners and enemies of God. The problem is, it's the truth. This is what we are by nature as we stand before God.

But notice how St Paul follows that up: *"While we were weak, at the right time Christ died for the ungodly..."* *"While we were still sinners, Christ died for us."* *"While we were enemies, we were reconciled to God by the death of His Son..."*

This is what the Grace of God is all about. It's nothing we deserve or can earn, but God in His love for us did what needed to be done in order that He could claim us as His own.

- *We are declared innocent before God by the blood of Christ. And through His death and resurrection, we are reconciled to God. And through our faith in Jesus Christ, we have eternal life and salvation. God's riches, at Christ's expense.*

Some things to think about:

Does St. Paul's statement that you are "weak, a sinner" and "an enemy of God" upset or offend you? Or does this knowledge help you begin to see the depths of love God has for you?

A lot of people would not be moved by the plight of their enemies. But God is. And since He was the only one who could do something about it, He did.

Even though you are "weak, a sinner" and "an enemy of God" it didn't matter what the "cost" was in order to make you His own, He willingly paid the price.

- **So now you are** *reconciled to God by the death of His Son."*

Let's Pray:

Heavenly Father, You are the God of grace and mercy who has reached out and made us Your own through the work of Jesus Christ. He is Your Son, and our Savior. We do not deserve Your love and forgiveness. And there is nothing we can do to earn it.

For all we can contribute to our salvation is sin. We are weak. And by our human nature we are Your enemies. But by the work of Your Son, you have overcome all that would separate us from You and made us Your own.

Help us to find in Your love and compassion the strength we need to believe that You are with us and carry us no matter the problems we face or the situations we find ourselves in. Some of us find ourselves surrounded by difficulties and struggles such as illness, financial uncertainty, loneliness, or isolation.

At such times it may be difficult to see Your love for us because our circumstances distract us. But help us to take comfort in Your grace and remember, as St Paul puts it, that we are *"reconciled to You through the death of Your Son."* And because we are reconciled, *"we will be saved by His life."* May we celebrate Your love for us all. In Jesus' name.

Amen

Chapter Nineteen

Jam'n Java
For the Soul
Book One

June 26

I think all of us have experienced times in our lives when we felt as if everything that could go wrong has gone wrong, and every enemy we have ever had is ganging up on us.

The Prophet Jeremiah lived in a time where he had been called by God to proclaim a message that wasn't very popular. In fact, it was often rejected, and he was persecuted for it.

Shortly after the death of Solomon, the kingdom of Israel was split into two nations: Israel to the north and Judah to the south.

As Jeremiah proclaims God's message, Israel has already been overrun by the Assyrians and the ten tribes that formed the nation of Israel were erased. Now, a little over 100 years later, a new bully has arisen; the Babylonians.

So, what do you do if you're the king of Judah? How do you face the certainty that they're going to come after you? Do you Surrender? Do you make an alliance with someone else? Judah chose to make an alliance with Egypt.

Jeremiah sees this invasion by Babylon not only as inevitable, but also the will of God.

You can imagine how popular that made him! The priests, the prophets and the nobility were all against him. And at one point he was arrested and imprisoned.

Put yourself in Jeremiah's position. What would you do? Jeremiah complained to God quite a bitterly. But he also trusted God.

In Jeremiah 20: 11-13 he writes,

But the **Lord** *is with me as a dread warrior; therefore, my persecutors will stumble; they will not overcome me.*

They will be greatly shamed, for they will not succeed.

Their eternal dishonor will never be forgotten.[12] O Lord of Hosts, who tests the righteous, who sees the heart and the mind, let me see your vengeance upon them, for to you have I committed my cause.

[13] Sing to the **Lord***; praise the* **Lord***! For he has delivered the life of the needy from the hand of evildoers.*

Jeremiah has been complaining a lot to God but notice what he does here: after the complaints he then states his trust in God to overcome the enemies he faces. Then he restates that trust by telling God, "to you I have committed my cause!"

And then he praises God as if everything he asked for is already an accomplished fact.
So, how are things going for you? Maybe it doesn't seem like the whole world is against you, but you may be discouraged or feeling down because of some of the things that are happening in your life.

I know some are facing health issues or maybe financial struggles. Maybe you're concerned about all the violence in our society and the world. Or maybe there is someone among your circle of friends and family that is having a difficult time.

There's a lot of stuff going on, isn't there? Instead of letting it get us down and discouraged, let's put it before the Lord God!

Some things to think about:

When life seems to present you with insurmountable problems, are you able to "look into the future" and see them as already solved? Not many of us are able to do that. Have you ever thought of God "being with you as a dread 'warrior?'" Why or why not? Even though the final victory may not look like you expect it to, but *"in all these things we are more than conquerors through Him who loved us." Romans 8:37*)

Let's Pray:

Father in heaven, You know the burdens of our hearts. You know our complaints and how dissatisfied we are with some things in our lives. You know our fears and our uncertainties.

We lay all of our garbage, all of that "stuff" that has us upset before you now. And we do so, Father, knowing that You are in control and will handle all of these problems, all of our uncertainties and whatever situation we find ourselves in.

You have already overcome all of our enemies through the death and resurrection of Your Son, Jesus Christ.

But sometimes it's difficult for us to see how that relates to our present life and situation. Help us to see the victories You win for us in every area of life. Give to us again the joy of our salvation.

We praise and glorify You for You have already overcome all of these problems we lay before You. Help us to celebrate not only tonight, but all of our lives. In Jesus' name.

Amen

Chapter Twenty

Jam'n Java
For the Soul

Book One

July 3

As I am writing this, we are in the midst of a very long 4th of July celebration! Last night, I watched an old documentary entitled, "The Boys of Company H". When I selected it, I thought it was a movie. As it turned out, it was a documentary about everything one Marine company experienced after they landed on Iwo Jima during World War II.

- *Let me begin by thanking all of you who are serving or have served in our nation's military, no matter which branch you were or are in. Thank you for your service.*

If I remember correctly, one of the observations made during this documentary about the Boys of Company H was that when they landed on Iwo Jima, their company consisted of 243 men.

- *When the battle ended, there were only 48 of them left. They had seen almost 200 of their friends and fellow soldiers killed.*

As you might expect, they were very emotional about what the flag meant to them. A couple of them said they would do it again, even given all that they now know about that battle. Which probably amazes all of us.

A couple of them commented, *"Freedom isn't free!"* And that's true, isn't it? ***Freedom isn't free, because someone else, or in this case, many "someones" laid down their life so you and I could experience the freedom we have today.***

As Americans, for over 200 years, men and women have stepped up and been willing to pay the price that our freedom requires.

- **As Christians, it was the blood of Jesus Christ, God's own Son, that purchased our freedom from sin. St. Paul writes in Galatians 5:1, *"For freedom Christ has set us free; stand firm therefore and do not submit again to a yoke of slavery."***

St. Paul is not thinking about political or national freedom, but the freedom we have as God's sons and daughters to love God, our brothers and sisters in Christ, and our neighbors.

There are many people in our nation who think of freedom in terms of what they can do. They think of freedom as how they can take advantage of opportunities they won't have in other countries. That's natural, I think.

But, maybe we should spend some time thinking about our freedom, not in terms of what we can do for ourselves, but in terms of how we can use our freedom for the benefit of others.

Some things to think about:

Jesus laid down His life for us. How can we use the freedom He has given us to serve one another?

_____

_____

_____

How can we lay down our lives for one another?

_____

_____

_____

How can we lay aside our self, our desires to help others meet their needs?

_____

_____

_____

That is true freedom!

Let's Pray:

Father, we live in a wonderful nation. It is not without its problems. We face injustice, hatred, greed and so many other things that we often refuse to address.

First, thank You for the freedom we have as Americans. But as wonderful as that freedom is, it pales in significance when compared to the freedom You have won for us through the blood of Jesus Christ.

Father, help us to live in that freedom and to refuse to submit to the yoke of slavery to sin.

Help us to live lives freed from greed, anger, hatred and self-centeredness.

Help us to live in love for You and one another.

We lift up those who are sick or suffering from illness. We pray for their healing.

We lift up our leaders and ask You to bless them as they lead our nation. But may they do so according to Your will and guidance. In Jesus' name.

Amen

Chapter
Twenty-One

JamnJava
For the Soul

Book One

July 10

This morning, I was thinking about some of the silly and dumb things I have done in the past.

Of course, the ones that stick with me and cause me the most difficulty and pain are the sins of the past.

Those are the ones that Satan keeps dragging up and showing me to convince me that I'm not the man I ought to be.

Maybe you've been at the point where you're feeling a lot of guilt and even grief over something you have done.

And you may have thought that what you have done is so bad it is impossible for God to forgive you and forgiveness is absolutely out of the question.

Remember Always: Grace and Mercy at the Cross!

If we seriously consider the totality of our lives, it is not just one incident, mistake, or sin we have to consider.

Someone once said if we actually knew the depth of our sin, and how offensive it is to God, we would go insane with despair.

Which makes what the Apostle Paul wrote in Ephesians 2, all the more powerful.

- *But God, being rich in mercy, because of the great love with which he loved us, even when we were dead in our trespasses, made us alive together with Christ - by grace you have been saved - and raised us up with him and seated us with him in the heavenly places in Christ Jesus,*

From time to time, I have heard people say, "You're dead to me!" to someone they are angry with. Just think about what that says about their relationship: it's gone, finished, over. Period. There's no way to reestablish or restore it.

Thank God that is not His response to us! Paul tells us when we were dead, because of our sin, God acted to make sure that our condition or situation was remedied. How? "He made us alive together with Christ!"

Do you get the image, the picture he's drawing? When Christ was raised from death, you and I were raised with Him. This is an act of God's grace and mercy. You and I have nothing to do with it and we contribute nothing to it!

How can God forgive you? How can He forgive me, or any of us, for all the things we have done that are contrary to His will? In Christ crucified!

He did it though Jesus, who was nailed to the cross, covered with our sin, and punished by God for what we have done. In Christ Jesus, we died with Him, were buried with Him, and are raised with Him. And Paul says, we are "seated with Him in heavenly places."

- ***Do you get it? By God's grace, and through His gift of faith, our salvation is already an accomplished fact! God already sees each of us seated in Heaven with Him.***

The answer to the question, "How can God forgive you and me?" is He has already forgiven us - long ago. He forgave us when His Son died on a cross, as our substitute, and rose victoriously over sin, death, and the accusations of the law against us! It's a done deal; an accomplished fact!

Some things to think about:

If you were to make a list of all the sins, mistakes and failures of your life, how long would that list be? Would you be able to remember everything you have done or failed to do? Picture yourself standing before the throne of heaven. God presents you with His list of everything you have ever done. As you look at the list you see these words stamped in red on that list: Paid In Full! That's what God has done for you!

Let's Pray:

Father, we don't understand the power of Your love and forgiveness. It is beyond our comprehension and in many ways, beyond our experience. It is not what we deserve.

But it is the way in which You have chosen to deal with us: mercy instead of justice and grace instead wrath.

Help us each day to live in Your grace and mercy and to love one another as You have loved us: with a sacrificial love and compassion.

Be with those who are heavy on our hearts this evening; those that are suffering from illness, loneliness and isolation, failed relationships, financial uncertainty or any of the other burdens our friends and loved ones carry.

Be with the doctors and nurses, our emergency medical technicians, police, firemen, military personnel. Protect them and keep them safe as they perform their duties of service to our community.

Guide and direct the leaders of our nation. We ask that You help us to glorify You in all that we do. In Jesus name.

Amen

Chapter
Twenty-Two

Jam'n Java
For the Soul

Book One

July 17

One of the Scripture reading for Sunday, July 16 was from Isaiah 55: verses 10-11.

as the rain and the snow come down from heaven
   and do not return there but water the earth, making it bring forth and sprout,
   giving seed to the Sower and bread to the eater,
¹¹ so shall my word be that goes out from my mouth;
   it shall not return to me empty,
but it shall accomplish that which I purpose,
   and shall succeed in the thing for which I sent it.

What is the purpose of the Word of God? You may have never thought about that because it's probably the kind of question only a pastor would ask! But God says His word will not return to Him empty and will accomplish the purpose for which He sent it!

So, what's the purpose of His word?

I think we would say it has many purposes, but only one goal. It often shows us where we have not lived up to the standards God has set for us.

Sometimes it encourages and strengthens us and helps us face whatever circumstances and situations we find ourselves in. Sometimes His word is a guide, as the Psalmist wrote, and a *"Lamp"* that lights our way. But there is only one goal: **to bring us to life and salvation.**

We don't have to look too far to find people who are willing to criticize what we have done or left undone. They are more than willing to find fault with us. Their purpose is not positive but destructive. They have very little interest in helping us improve.

When the Word of God shows us our failures it isn't to destroy us but to restore us. It isn't to reject us, but to assure us that He loves us, and His arms are open to us to comfort and reassure us.

Sometimes the consequences of what we have done are very real, but they aren't the ultimate truth. Sometimes the criticisms leveled against us are built on a small foundation of truth, but they are not the ultimate verdict. No, the ultimate verdict comes from Him who sent His Son to suffer and die for us. The ultimate truth is that in Christ Jesus, no matter what we have done, we are forgiven. Whatever is bothering us, whatever is troubling us, it's okay!

God has already taken care of it in the cross of Jesus and the empty tomb!

- *You and I are going to make it because He's going to bring us through it! That's His Word of promise to all who believe in Jesus Christ. And His Word accomplishes everything for which He has designed it.*

Some things to think about:

Which source of criticism is the most difficult for you to deal with: that from without (from others) or that from within (from yourself)?

_____

_____

_____

_____

_____

_____

_____

Does the idea that the purpose of criticism from fellow human beings, is not positive, but rather destructive, give you a "tool" to handle it?

_____

_____

_____

How do you know whether the criticism from fellow human beings is valid?

_____

_____

_____

Does the idea that the ultimate verdict and the ultimate truth depends only on what God says about us help you to deal with the critical people (including yourself) you find in your life?

_____

_____

_____

Let's Pray:

Father in heaven, we ask for Your blessing even as some of us struggle with circumstances and situations that seem beyond our control.

Those struggles may be a result of our health, or our finances, or our relationships with other people.

Sometimes life just seems to take delight in beating us down and trying to drive us to despair.

Help us to take comfort in your word of promise, your word of life.

Strengthen our faith and trust in You so that we can look past whatever trouble and uncertainties today presents us with to the victories that lie in the future through Your grace and mercy.

Reassure us we are forgiven, righteous and free because of Christ alone. In Jesus' name we ask this.

Amen

Chapter
Twenty-Three

Jam'n Java
For the Soul
Book One

August 7

The Old Testament Lesson for August 6 was from Isaiah 55. Verses 1 to 3 read:

- *"Come, everyone who thirsts, come to the waters; and he who has no money, come, buy and eat!*
Come, buy wine and milk without money and without price.
Why do you spend your money for that which is not bread, and your labor for that which does not satisfy?
Listen diligently to me, and eat what is good, and delight yourselves in rich food.
Incline your ear, and come to me; hear, that your soul may live;
and I will make with you an everlasting covenant, my steadfast, sure love for David.

It's obvious that we live in a world that is "thirsty," as people try to quench their thirst with drugs, alcohol, power, control, wealth, or pleasure. Any or all of that just to try to satisfy that thirst or fill that void, a sense of emptiness we all seem to have.

Christians also experience a sense of thirst at times. There are points in our lives in which we are uncertain about things; where life is going, which path to take, why things have happened in the way they have. It's at those times or those moments when we have questions that this sense of "thirst" develops within us.

- ***There is a gracious invitation from God in these words, "Come, everyone who thirsts, come to the waters; and he who has no money, come, buy and eat! Come, buy wine and milk without money and without price,***

There's a part of me that wants to ask, "How can you buy and eat when you don't have any money? That's not the way the world works!"

Instead of thinking in terms of buying and selling, I'd like to suggest we think in terms of investing – Investing in "wine and milk that has no price."

In other words, "wine and milk" that are ours for the taking. And what "wine and milk" would that be?

You probably know where I'm going with this. In John 6:35 Jesus tells His disciples and those that are following Him,

"I am the bread of life; whoever comes to me shall not hunger, and whoever believes in me shall never thirst.

There's a hymn that we used to sing when I was growing up. I love it. We usually sang it when the offering was being gathered. You may not know it, but it was "Take My Life and Let it Be."

Don't worry about it, I'm not going to sing it! But I do want to share some of the verses with you:

Take my life and let it be, consecrated Lord to Thee;
Take my moments and my days, let them flow in ceaseless praise.
Take my hands and let them move At the impulse of Thy love;
Take my feet and let the be, swift and beautiful for Thee.
Take my voice and let me sing, Always, only, for my King,
Take my lips and let them be, filled with messages from Thee.

All you and I have to "invest" in the Lord, to "buy and eat," is ourselves. All I have to give Jesus, is me - my heart, my soul, my strength and my mind. Is it too much to ask of me? Is it too much to ask of you?

A little later in John 6 we are told that a lot of people who had been following Jesus decided to walk away. They didn't like what He was teaching. It was too much! John tells us that Jesus turned to the twelve and asked them if they, too, wanted to leave Him. Peter responded for them, and this is one of the times he got it right. He said, *"Lord, to whom shall we go? You have the words of eternal life!"*

As I mentioned earlier; all of us have times of uncertainty and questions about where life is taking us. But we also know Him who is the **Bread of Life.** We know Him who is the living water. We know Him who gave up His life for us, and has pledged Himself to us and told us, *"Never will I leave you. Never will I forsake you."*

Wherever you are this evening, whatever you're going though, Hear the invitation again:

"Come, to the waters...come, buy and eat! Come, buy wine and milk without money and without price. Listen .... and eat what is good and delight yourselves in rich food. Incline your ear, and come... hear, that your soul may live; and I will make with you an everlasting covenant, my steadfast, sure love for David.

Some things to think about:

How "thirsty" are you right now? What are you thirsty for?

_____

_____

_____

Someone once observed that the only things we can hold onto are the things we give away. What emotions do you experience when someone says, "Give everything to Jesus!"?

_____

_____

_____

What "empty places" in your life would you like the Lord to "fill" for you?

_____

_____

_____

Let's Pray:

Father in heaven, fill the empty places of our lives with Your Holy Spirit. Bring healing to the wounds we have suffered.

Some of those wounds are self-induced, and some of them have been inflicted by the events of life or other people.

We live in a world filled with doubt and skepticism. And sometimes we are restless with uncertainty.

But as Peter said, where else can we go Father, but to You? You sent us Your Son as our Savior. He has the words that lead to eternal life. Indeed, He IS your Word of life. He is the Living Water.

Help us to come to You, Father, through Your Son Jesus, that we may receive all the blessings of life and salvation You have promised us.

Grant us that peace which surpasses all understanding. Take our lives and let them glorify You in all that we do. In Jesus' name.

Amen

Chapter
Twenty-Four

Jam'nJava
For the Soul
Book One

August 13

The Epistle lesson for August 12 was Romans 10:5-17. I'd like to share verses 9 through 13 with you.

…if you confess with your mouth that Jesus is Lord and believe in your heart that God raised him from the dead, you will be saved. [10] For with the heart one believes and is justified, and with the mouth one confesses and is saved. [11] For the Scripture says, "Everyone who believes in him will not be put to shame."[12] For there is no distinction between Jew and Greek; for the same Lord is Lord of all, bestowing his riches on all who call on him. [13] For "everyone who calls on the name of the Lord will be saved."

As I study this passage I am unsure which portion of it I should focus on. Do I focus on confession? Do I focus on faith? Do I talk about justification? Or do I discuss the faithfulness of God? Of course, I could discuss all of those topics which might create a devotional so long (and complex) you might not finish it.

Let me start here; "Everyone who calls on the name of the Lord will be saved." St Paul is actually quoting the Old Testament Prophet Joel (2:32). It reminds me that the way of salvation has always rested in the Lord our God.

God's plan has never been to save some and cast off others. John 3:16 reminds us of God's love for all mankind as the Apostle writes, *"For God so loved the world that he gave his only Son, that whoever believes in Him should not perish but have everlasting life."*

He loved the world. He didn't love some people, or most people; He loves all. But there is a problem.

- **We are all broken people, stained with the rebellion of our first parents.**

We have not, and indeed cannot, live up to the demand for righteousness made by God. We are not what we are supposed to be. Even the best of us falls short of what God demands.

- In verse 12 St Paul says, *"there is no distinction between Jew and Greek…"*

We love distinctions, don't we! How many times have we heard people say, or thought to ourselves, "Well, at least I've never done that!" Or maybe it's phrased this way; "I have my faults, but I never _____!"

I don't know how you would fill in that blank. I could say I've never committed murder, but Jesus said if I hate someone that's the same thing as murder. I could say I've never committed adultery, but Jesus said lusting after a woman is the same thing.

I could say I've never stolen, but coveting someone else's property is tantamount to committing the sin, because what goes on in our heart is just as important as what we actually do publicly.

Jesus points this out in Matthew 15:19: ***For out of the heart come evil thoughts, murder, adultery, sexual immorality, theft, false witness, slander.***

Do you see the connection between heart and action (sin)? Generally, our sins are not something which generally just "happen." Often, we've been thinking about it in some way shape or form. The thought, produced by desire or envy, plants a seed in our heart. And that seed takes root and produces our sins. Recognizing this is why verse 10 is so very beautiful and powerful for us.

- ***"For with the heart one believes and is justified, and with the mouth one confesses and is saved."***

The Holy Spirit plants faith in our hearts, and that faith takes root, and it produces the kind of fruit God desires. In this passage St. Paul points to the act of confession of ***Jesus as our Savior and Lord.*** It is by this gift of faith that we are put right with God. And by that I mean we become what God wants us to be, in every aspect of our lives.

We live in an age where medical practices are doing astounding things. Perhaps you or a loved one has benefited from some of these "miracles." Maybe someone you know, or love has had a heart transplant, or a kidney transplant. These are often lifesaving procedures.

May I suggest to you that you and I have benefited from a more significant and powerful "lifesaving procedure," the death and resurrection of Jesus Christ. In our baptism we were buried with Him and when the Father raised Him from the dead, so we were raised with Him. Our faith ties us to Jesus not only in the present, but into the future and into eternity. So that *"whoever calls on the name of the Lord will be saved."*

Some things to think about:

It might seem a bit overly dramatic to suggest we have received a *"heart transplant"* through our faith in Christ, but the Apostle Paul indicates the miracle worked by God through the Holy Spirit is far more extensive when he writes in 2 Corinthians 5:17: *if anyone is in Christ, he is a new creation. The old has passed away; behold, the new has come."*

Maybe you also experience some of the same doubts and uncertainties I do from time to time.

I look at my failures in life, not just my shortcomings, not only the sins everyone knows about, but the ones no one has discovered. I know God knows about them.

Do you do what I often do and wonder how God can put up with you?

Do you ever question your salvation because when you look at yourself all you see are your weaknesses and failures?

What's the answer to this struggle?

- ***The answer is to stop looking at ourselves and to look to Jesus instead.***

We are never going to measure up against what we should be (or must be).

Trying to do this is only going to produce doubt and uncertainty. Looking to Jesus shows us how God has solved our problem. He took our failures and weaknesses on Himself and gave us His righteousness through our faith.

In Him we are absolutely what we are supposed to be, even when we fail. Because all our failures were taken care of at the cross.

Let's Pray:

Father in heaven, there are so many ways in which we struggle with our sinful condition. Sometimes we are buried beneath a mountain of guilt and pain. Sometimes all we can see is our failure.

Help us to turn our eyes away from ourselves and, as the old hymn says, to "turn our eyes upon Jesus." Help us to focus on what He has done for us.

Help us to understand that all our sins have been forgiven through the faith You Yourself have given us.

Produce within us the desire to serve You and one another more fully and completely. Help us to trust the promises You have given us through Your Word. In Jesus name we pray.

Amen

Chapter
Twenty-Five

Jam'n Java
For the Soul
Book One

September 4

Earlier today I was thinking about the Apostle Paul and some of the things he experienced as an Apostle. Just reading the list of things he experienced causes me a great deal of amazement at his faith and trust in the Lord. He endured beatings, rejection, attempts on his life, he was cast adrift in the ocean, and was shipwrecked,

And yet, in spite of having experienced all of these things, there was one other thing that seemed to bother him even more. He writes about it in 2 Corinthians 12. This is verses 7 through 10:

- *So to keep me from becoming conceited because of the surpassing greatness of the revelations, a thorn was given me in the flesh, a messenger of Satan to harass me, to keep me from becoming conceited. Three times I pleaded with the Lord about this, that it should leave me. But he said to me, "My grace is sufficient for you, for my power is made perfect in weakness." Therefore I will boast all the more gladly of my weaknesses, so that the power of Christ may rest upon me. For the sake of Christ, then, I am content with weaknesses, insults, hardships, persecutions, and calamities. For when I am weak, then I am strong."*

I know some of you might be going through really difficult things. And you didn't tune in to *Jam' n Java* this evening to be reminded of them. And that old bit of advice, ***"Everyone is going through some kind of problem, some difficulty, something they are struggling with"*** doesn't help either.

I only bring this up, because I'm in the same boat. It's not a cliché to say that all of us are going through our own struggles and difficulties. But I don't bring it up to say something like, ***"Get over it! You're not the only one facing difficulties!"*** Or ***"You've got to pull yourself up by your bootstraps!"*** When you're going through difficult times, those things are offensive.

When I am going through a rough time, these words of our Lord to St. Paul, are of great comfort to me. ***"My grace is sufficient for you, for my power is made perfect in weakness."*** That's really what the Christian life is all about – the sufficiency of the grace of God.

His promise is good no matter what problems or difficulties we are going through. And I hope these words of the Lord speak to you this evening no matter what difficulty you are going through at this moment; no matter where you are struggling or the questions you have tonight.

No matter how great the mountain in front of us appears to be, God's grace will be sufficient for you and for me...just as it was for the Apostle. We are going to make it through all of this. Our Lord has promised His power is made perfect even in the midst of our weaknesses. His grace is sufficient!

Some things to think about:

What specific problems, difficulties, or "impossible mountains" lie before you?

_____

_____

_____

_____

How difficult is it to be "content" in your weaknesses, hardships and problems?

_____

_____

_____

_____

Reach out and ask the Lord to give you His strength in the midst of your weakness.

Let's Pray:

Father in heaven, how beautiful are the promises Your word gives us! How great are your assurances to lift us up and strengthen us in the midst of our struggles and the conflicts and uncertainties we face.

You know our fears. You know how broken and wounded we are Father. We are broken and wounded, not just because of our problems and difficulties caused by life, but because of our own sins as well.

Help us to find comfort and strength through the promise of Your grace, no matter what our struggles might be and no matter what the circumstances, situations, or our fears might be.

Grant us the faith to put our trust in Your promises, and to experience Your perfect power even in the midst of our weakness. And help us to live in the sufficiency of Your grace in all things. In Jesus' name.

Amen

Chapter
Twenty-Six

Jam'n Java
For the Soul

Book One

September 11

I suppose most of us took some time to reflect on the fact that it is September 11th and remembered the attacks which took place 22 years ago today. It doesn't seem possible that it has been that long.

All of us can remember what we were doing and what we felt and experienced on that day when we first heard about the attacks.

My wife was in the St. Louis area spending some time with her mother. She was supposed to return home on that day and called me and told me, "They're flying airplanes into buildings in New York."

To which I responded with my usual skepticism, and she told me to turn on the television. And when I did, I discovered it was all too true.

I can't begin to imagine the fear, anxiety, uncertainty and grief those of you who live on the East Coast went through on that day and the following days. Some of you lost family members or close friends. And one of the things we lost as a nation was our sense of security.

As I think back on that time this seems kind of arrogant. We had this attitude that we were safe and secure because no other nation had ever been able to attack us on our soil.

And I don't think we understood how much hatred there is in the world, just in general, but also directed against us as a nation.

My wife was supposed to fly back to California on September 11, but we all remember how travel restrictions were quickly imposed. Since she couldn't return, she went back and spent the rest of the day with her mother, who then was called home by the Lord the next day.

As tragic and uncertain as September 11th was for her, there was still a blessing in it, because her mother came out of a coma, and she and my wife were able to have one last conversation before the Lord called her mother home.

As I said before, I know a lot of you went through a lot of pain and uncertainty on that day 22 years ago. Some of you might resent the fact that I even bring it up, because of the pain you experienced, and you don't want to go through it again.

I understand that, and I don't bring it up to drag you through all of those emotions, heart ache and pain. I bring it up to make this point: Evil is a constant threat in our lives. I know we would like to believe that it's possible for all of us to get along. But it isn't.

- *Why can't we all get along? Because we're all human. We're all broken, we're all fallible, and even though we don't like the word, we're all sinners. In addition to this we also have an enemy that we would like to ignore or believe doesn't exist: Satan. And for those of us who are in Christ, he will do all he can to make us doubt, or to question God's love for us.*

It's become popular among a certain segment of our society, to ask the question, **"Where is God?"** when bad things or evil things happen. Usually it's asked, *"How can a good God let bad things happen?"* Which, if you think about it, is kind of like me blaming my wife when I can't find my car keys because I put them someplace I normally don't. God isn't responsible because I decide to do some evil thing to another person or a group of people.

But there's another answer, one that we often forget or don't think of. Where was God? Where is God? Where He has always been. As St. Paul writes in 2 Corinthians 5:19, *God was in Christ, reconciling the world to Himself.*

Maybe I can say it this way: Where was God when this evil or that evil was committed? Where was God when this sin was committed against us, or these terrible things were done to us either as a nation or as individuals?

189

The answer is...He was where He has always been, right beside us. This is what the cross is all about. This is what the suffering of Christ is all about. All the evil of the world, everything done to or by us was heaped up on Jesus, so that by His suffering and death, we might be reconciled to God. And reconciled to one another.

Some things to think about:

Reflecting on your life, what are some of the "evils" you have experienced and have you been able to come to grips with this evil?

_____

_____

_____

It's always easier to think about the things done "to" us and much easier to forget what we have done to others. What are some things you have done to hurt or offend others? Can you go to them and ask for forgiveness?

_____

_____

_____

Let's Pray:

Father in heaven, there is so much evil in this world. There is so much suffering, pain, and heartache. We don't understand the profound hatred that is so often revealed in this world. There seems to be no excuse for it and yet it exists. We cannot comprehend it.

Sometimes You are accused of not caring about all of this evil because people don't see an immediate reaction from You. And yet, You have shown us where Your heart is. You have shown us what You think about us. You have given us Your answer in the suffering and death of Your Son, Jesus.

In His death and resurrection, You have made it possible for us to be reconciled not only to You, but to one another. By Your love for us, You have made it possible for us to love one another. Help us to trust You in all things and to understand that You have already overcome evil and have given us the victory in all things.

Comfort those who grieve and mourn. Strengthen the weak among us. And help us to see that no matter what happens to us, You are with us. In Jesus name.

Amen

Chapter
Twenty-Seven

Jam'n Java
For the Soul
Book One

September 18

I appeal to you therefore, brothers,
by the mercies of God, to present your
bodies as a living sacrifice, holy and acceptable
to God, which is your spiritual
worship. ²Do not be conformed to this world, but
be transformed by the renewal of
your mind, that by testing you may
discern what is the will of God, what is good and
acceptable and perfect. (Romans 12:1-2 esv)

Chuck Swyndol once observed, ***"The problem***
with a living sacrifice is that it wants to crawl off
the altar." I've often wondered what was going
through Isaac's mind when Abraham told him he
was the sacrifice God required. I imagine there was
a whole lot of fear, but we aren't told whether he
said anything or not.

By the mercies of God, St. Paul says, what mercy?
Not the good things of life that you and I enjoy every
day. Or the times that He has pulled us out of what
seems to be impossible situations or
circumstances.

But the mercy by which Isaac was a picture of what
God Himself would do for us. As God asked
Abraham to offer up His own son, God would offer
His Son as a ransom for each and every one of us.

This is the mercy by which God's own Son crawled up on the altar, the cross, in order that He might be the living sacrifice for us.

As I was thinking about this, it struck me that the greatest words of the Gospel are these two: for you!

It's one thing to hear that Jesus offered Himself as the ransom for sin and there is forgiveness available to us. It's quite another to hear this was done, for you, and the forgiveness is, for you.

In our practice of the Lord's Supper, as the bread and wine are distributed, we are told, *"this is the body of Christ, the blood of Christ, shed for the forgiveness of sin, for you."*

"So," St. Paul writes, "in light of what God has done, for you, present your body as a living sacrifice."

But I still have a problem, and I imagine you have the same one. It's the one I mentioned earlier: my human nature doesn't want to get up on the altar. Or, as Jesus put it, I don't want to deny myself. I don't want to pick up my cross and follow Him.

I don't want to be a living sacrifice. What I want is to follow, when it's convenient or when it doesn't get in my way.

I recently heard someone describe the Christian life in this way:

- *It's, sin, sin, sin and repent, repent, repent and try to love your neighbor.*

How many times do we get frustrated with our inability to live as we think God wants us to live?

Which of your sins did Jesus die for?

Some of them? Most of them?

Or…all of them, past, present and future?

- *When Jesus got up on the cross, He did everything you and I need so we might be, holy and acceptable to God.*

We've got nothing to do with it. Jesus has done it all for us. You are a person upon whom God has poured out this mercy.

And through Jesus and through your faith, you are holy and acceptable to God, and because you're being transformed you can see yourself differently, as holy and acceptable before God, through Christ Jesus.

And we have the Word of God to tell us what the good and perfect will of God is.

Some things to think about:

What do you think was going through Isaac's mind when his father Abraham told him he was going to be sacrificed to God?

_____

_____

_____

What do you think you would be thinking about if you were told you would be sacrificed to God?

_____

_____

_____

How important are the words "for you" in the Gospel?

_____

_____

_____

Let's Pray:

Father, help us to see ourselves as You see us; as Your redeemed Children, holy and acceptable to You.

Help us to see this is not because of what we have done, but because of what You have done for us in the person of Jesus Christ.

As frustrated as we are by our weaknesses and failures, help us to see the power of Your love for us as it is spoken to us.

Help us to see that this forgiveness, renewal and mercy is for us; for each one of us!

Heal the sick and ill and be with those who are heavy on our hearts. Bless the proclamation of the Gospel. In Jesus' name.

Amen

Chapter
Twenty-Eight

Jam'n Java
For the Soul
Book One

September 25

I hope this day has been good to you. But having said that, every day presents us with some good things, as well as some things that are not so good. And some days it seems difficult for us to maintain a positive perspective, no matter how much we try.

That might be because of something someone has done to us, or it might be as a result of something we have done, and the results are not what we wanted or expected.

In fact, they may have turned out disastrous. And sometimes, things happen just because that's the way life is and there's no explanation to help us understand why this thing happened. Sometimes the only answer we get is, "*Life isn't fair. It can be downright cruel!*"

Well, with that bit of joyful comment, I'd like to share a portion of Isaiah 55:

Isaiah writes:

> *"Seek the Lord while he may be found; call upon him while he is near;*

> *let the wicked forsake his way, and the unrighteous man his thoughts;*

let him return to the Lord, that he may have compassion on him,

and to our God, for he will abundantly pardon"

Isaiah was prophet to people who didn't want to hear what God had to say.

They were going through the motions of worship and obedience to God, but their hearts were far from God.

I'd like to assume that you and I are in a completely different place in terms of our relationship to God.

- *But is that a safe assumption? Is there nothing in our lives that is contrary to the will of God? Are there no thoughts or attitudes that are unrighteous?*

The usual thing we do is to rationalize this stuff. We say, "Well, I'm not as bad as 'so and so'". Or "Well, at least I've never done – fill in the blank. But that's not the point, is it?

Scripture is very clear that our failure before God is not only in what we have done, or said, but also in our thoughts and attitudes.

We have also failed in not doing the things that we should have done.

- *Here's the point: all of us need to return to the Lord.*
  I'd like to think that I never left Him. And yet, I'm just like the Apostle Paul as he says in Romans,

"The good I want to do I don't do and the evil I don't want to do is what I do."

Isaiah says to us, *return to the Lord, that he may have compassion on us, and to our God, for he will abundantly pardon"*

Someone once said that the first words God hears are, "Lord, have mercy."

This is good for us to remember, no matter what our situation or circumstances might be, whether we are in good or difficult times, or whether we are rejoicing or filled with sorrow and pain.

Why?

- *Because, as Isaiah says, the Lord has compassion, and He will abundantly pardon all those who turn to Him.*

And St. Paul, after describing what an absolute failure he is, writes, "Thanks be to God who delivers me through Jesus Christ our Lord."

That's what the cross and the empty grave are all about. God has taken upon Himself the debt you and I have and could never pay for ourselves. But He has redeemed each and every one of us through Jesus. And it is through Him that God does have compassion and mercy, and through Him we have the abundant pardon Isaiah talks about.

Some things to think about:

How easily do the difficulties of life keep you from, **"Seek(ing) the Lord while He may be found?"**

It's very popular in our society to assume if things don't go as we want or expect them to go, God is picking on us, or doesn't care about us.

How easily do you fall into that trap?

_____

_____

_____

It might be helpful to think of all the things you have done wrong, especially those things only you and God know about. Take a sheet of paper and make a list of them. Then, after "Seeking the Lord," burn the list and know, He has compassion, and will abundantly pardon you. Your sins are gone, and you are redeemed though Christ our Lord.

Let's Pray:

Lord, have mercy. Have mercy on each and every one of us.

Some of us come before you in discouragement and pain because of the events of life, which can be so cruel.

Some of us come before You because of illness or disease.

Some of us come in sorrow because we have lost loved ones due to death.

Some of us come to You facing danger and uncertainty because we serve and put our lives on the line for others.

Again, we pray, Lord have mercy. Comfort those who mourn and reassure those who are facing difficult circumstances and situations.

Assure us that no matter what we face, You are near to us and hear us. Help us to see in Christ crucified that we are forgiven, redeemed and cherished by You. May we glorify You in all that we do. In Jesus' name.

Amen

Chapter
Twenty-Nine

Jam'n Java
For the Soul
Book One

October 2

I'd like to share a couple of thoughts with you based on St. Paul's letter to the Philippians, Chapter 1:6 –

"And I am sure of this, that He who began a good work in you will bring it to completion at the day of Jesus Christ."

Every Christian goes though periods of doubt and uncertainty in life. It's only natural. After all, life is filled with all kinds of negative people and events. On one hand, we sometimes get criticized for not being more like Jesus.

And on the other hand, we get criticized for thinking we're better than other people.

And if that's not enough, there are the kinds of things that happen in life, such as illness, that cause us to pause and reflect. And sometimes we ask the question, *"Why me?"* And we haven't even begun to talk about our own human weaknesses and failures yet.

I don't know about you, but during these times of uncertainty, it sometimes becomes easy for me to doubt my relationship to God. Not from the aspect of His love for me but from the aspect of my love and obedience toward Him.

After all, if I really do love God with all my heart, soul, strength and mind, wouldn't I be able to see it in my own thoughts, and words and actions? Wouldn't I be able to see some growth, some positive change in my life?

At the root of those questions is a false assumption; a lie that permeates our humanity: and that lie is that somehow, in some way, my relationship to God depends on what I can or have or will do. In this one little verse St. Paul blows that whole thought and attitude apart.

If I were to ask you, "**What is the one thing God wants from you?**" what would your answer be?

_____

_____

_____

Scripture tells us that the answer to that question is faith. Hebrews 11:6 tells us that without faith it is impossible to please God. But what is faith and how do you get it?

First of all it's God's gift to you and me. We receive it through the work of the Holy Spirit who helps us put our trust in Jesus Christ.

Not only for our salvation, but in all things, including those times of doubt and uncertainty. Paul says he is confident that, *"He who began a good work in you."* This "good work" is not something you or I do, begin, or decide. It is something God has begun in us.

- *And what is that good work? Our faith. Or we could say our salvation?*

What about our Salvation? God *"will bring it to completion on the day of Jesus Christ."*

We need to understand the full implications of the fact that our relationship with God, from beginning to completion is totally and completely the work of God.

- *We contribute nothing to it.*

And we also need to remember we are not a finished project.

One day we will be, on the day of Jesus Christ, when He returns. But until then, we are not, thank God what we once were, but we also are not what we are going to be.

God began our faith and our relationship to Him. And God will bring it to completion. In between, nothing will separate us from His love and mercy.

Some things to think about:

To our human logic it just doesn't seem like faith can be enough to keep us in good standing with God. But the book of Isaiah tells us that all our righteousness (all the good things we do) is as "filthy rags" before God.

If that is true, how can faith be enough to please God?

_____

_____

_____

How does the good news that this is not dependent on anything you or I do, but that God has already begun this "good work" in you, help you understand the power of God's love for you?

_____

_____

_____

Let's Pray:

Father in heaven, You know how the uncertainties of life can plague us and cause us to question our relationship to you.

The system of the world around us, the evil one, and even our own human nature points out our failures before You. They seek to create doubt in our hearts and minds in order to ruin our relationship to You and destroy our faith.

But that faith and relationship is not contingent upon what they say, it is contingent upon Your Word of promise.

And You have promised that You will never leave us or forsake us. No matter our situation or circumstances tonight, help us trust Your Word and promise. Help us to know that no matter what we are going through, it is not Your final Word to us.

Help us to look forward to that day when You will bring it all to completion and we will see ourselves as You see us: as the redeemed and perfect children You have created us to be in Your Son, Christ Jesus. It is in His name that we pray.

Amen

Chapter Thirty

Jam'n Java
For the Soul
Book One

October 9

Yesterday was the nineteenth Sunday after Pentecost, and the epistle lesson was from Philippians 3.

In the lesson St. Paul mentions all of what we might call the "spiritual advantages" he had as a Jew. But he rejected them and cast them aside because of the surpassing value of knowing Christ Jesus and having a righteousness in Him that comes through faith.

Then he adds this: ***"Not that I have already obtained this or am already perfect, but I press on to make it my own, because Christ Jesus has made me his own. ¹³ Brothers, I do not consider that I have made it my own. But one thing I do: forgetting what lies behind and straining forward to what lies ahead, ¹⁴ I press on toward the goal for the prize of the upward call of God in Christ Jesus."***

It's easy to get caught up in the daily things of life, isn't it? We have things to do, places to go, and needs that must be met. And as we go about the various activities of life and meeting those demands, it's easy to forget who we are and who we belong to.

More specifically, it's easy, at least for me, to forget that we live by faith and not by sight, to quote the Apostle Paul again.

We know that not everything is going to go the way we want it to or think it ought to in life. We're going to make mistakes and fail. And it's easy to get angry at a wrong done to us or become frustrated over our circumstances or our situation.

There are times when I reflect on my past sins and failures and wonder how it is that God can ever forgive me for those things.

I know the answer, at least intellectually. But deep down inside there are the persistent accusations of guilt and shame. One of those accusations is that I do not deserve the love and mercy of God.

And you know that accusation is all too true. None of us deserve the love and mercy of God. But here's the thing; It's not about what you or I deserve or have earned, it's about what we have been given.

This is what St. Paul is talking about when he says, ***forgetting what lies behind and straining forward to what lies ahead, 14 I press on toward the goal for the prize of the upward call of God in Christ Jesus."***

Forgetting what lies behind: forgetting all the failures and mistakes, forgetting all the injuries, insults, forgetting all the wrongs done to us and striving forward to what lies ahead.

- ***That's the goal.***

St. Paul says something else I think is important to us: He says, "***I press on to make it my own, because Christ Jesus has made me his own.***"

St. Paul says He recognizes his own failures and inconsistencies, but he presses on to be the man God called him to be, because Christ Jesus made him His own. And beloved, Christ Jesus has made you His own as well.

So, whatever your vocation might be, whatever you find yourself doing in this day-to-day life, try to remember you belong to Jesus and He has claimed you as His own.

None of us is perfect, but we are forgiven, through our faith in Christ Jesus, to whom we belong.

Some things to think about:

What is the difference between the "pressing on" St. Paul describes and the attempt to "earn salvation" which is so commonly accepted in our society?

What is the "goal" St. Paul is "pressing on" toward?

How can we truly "forget what lies behind" when we have so many failures and weaknesses in the past?

What does God say about the past when we come to faith in Christ?

Let's Pray:

Father in heaven, how good and gracious you are to us. We have no claim upon your mercy or forgiveness, other than through the work of the Holy Spirit, where we have been claimed through your Son and belong to Him. Help us to remember who we are in the day-to-day routines of life. Do not allow either the failures or the successes of the past to diminish our zeal or determination to reach the goal set before us: the prize of the upward call of Christ.

Some of us face difficulties that seem impossible to resolve; some with illnesses or disease; some with personal relationships that are strained; some with financial insecurity; some with uncertainty about their future. Help us all to remember we have been claimed by You, through Your Son, Jesus Christ. And although the immediate future may seem uncertain to us, it is not to You. You know where we are going because You are leading us. And ultimately, we will be, with You. Thank You again Father, for all your goodness to us. In Jesus' name.

Amen

Chapter
Thirty-One

Jam'n Java
For the Soul

Book One

October 23

Yesterday I had the privilege of filling in for Pastor Robert Lyon Barker at Trinity Lutheran Church in Simi Valley, California. My sermon was based on the Gospel lesson from Matthew 22:15-22 where Jesus' enemies were trying to trap Him in His words so they could get him killed.

They ask him if it is legal, according to Jewish religious laws, to pay taxes to Caesar. It's not really a question about paying taxes. It's an ingenious attempt to discredit him and possibly have him killed by the Romans.

If He says it is legal or proper to pay the taxes, He loses favor with the people who hated the Roman occupation.

If He says it isn't legal, He's in danger of being charged with sedition by the Romans.

- ***It's what we might call a "gotcha-question."***

On the surface of things, it seems whichever way Jesus answers, He's going to be in trouble!

But Jesus is aware of their malice and asks to see one of the coins for the tax. They show him a Roman coin called a denarius.

Jesus asks them whose image and inscription are on the coin. They answer it is "Caesar's."

Jesus told them to give to Caesar the things that belong to Ceasar and give to God the things that belong to God.

On the surface, that's not only a clever escape from the trap they set for him, it also appears to be a neat and clean way to separate things to serve God and the government properly.

Some people might say it this way, "Spiritual things on Sunday, secular things on Monday through Saturday." *Of course, here in America, we would say, "Don't confuse the separation of Church and state!"*

But what is it that we owe God?

How do we give to God the things that belong to God?

In 1 Corinthians 6:19b-20 St Paul writes *"You are not your own, you were bought with a price."* He's referring to is the sacrifice of Jesus on the cross. Through His death we were bought, purchased and redeemed. However, you wish to say it. That's what St. Paul means when he says we were bought with a price. I am not my own, I belong to God.

Everything that I am. My life, my talents, my body, soul, spirit, strength, mind, heart, and intellect. Everything belongs to Jesus.

It's not as simple as Spiritual things for Sunday and secular things for every other day of the week.

- *Giving to God what belongs to God is a complicated day-by-day, hour-by-hour, minute-by-minute and second-by-second proposition.*

I don't know about you, but I'm not very consistent at that!

When Jesus went to the cross for us, all of our sins were nailed to that cross with Him.

By Jesus' death He made peace with God on our behalf.

The theological jargon for that is the term *reconciliation.* We are reconciled to God. Another way to say it is through Christ we are back in a favorable relationship with God and nothing can take that away.

St. Paul also explains 1 Corinthians 11:6, *"you were washed, you were sanctified, you were justified in the name of the Lord Jesus Christ and by the Spirit of our God.*

I don't have the time or space here to go into that completely but just let me say it this way: **You are everything God wants you to be because He has accomplished it in you in Jesus Christ.**

It has nothing to do with what you or I can do for God. It is all about what he's done through the work of the Holy Spirit. He has cleansed you and consecrated you for Himself. He has made you righteous in His sight. Through Jesus.

And yes, we still have our weaknesses and failures before God. I'm still a sinner and I'm still struggling. But I'm a forgiven sinner, and so are you, through the salvation won for us in the life, death and resurrection of our Lord Jesus Christ. As the song says, I am His, and He is mine!

Some things to think about:

Have you ever been in a situation in which it seemed no matter what you did, it was the wrong thing?

_____

_____

_____

Forgive the "earthy language" but it's sometimes referred to as, "Damned if you do, and damned if you don't!" Satan loves to snare us into "impossible" situations where all the choices we have seem "bad." Look back on the bad times in your life.

What did God do to bring you victory and get you out of the predicament you were in?

_____

_____

_____

What did you learn about yourself?

_____

_____

_____

What did you learn about God?

_____

_____

_____

Let's Pray:

Father in heaven, thank you for making each of us Your children and claiming us as Your own.

There are days when we struggle with our identity as Your children, Father.

These are the days when we don't see in ourselves the kind of things we know should be evident if we really belong to You.

Help us to recognize that it is not about us and what we can do, but about You and what You have done for us through our Savior, Jesus.

Be with those whom we name before you in our hearts, who are suffering from illness or disease, discouragement, frustration or doubt.

Be with the doctors who minister to the sick. Protect those who serve to protect us within our society.

And may all that we do, glorify you. In Jesus' name.

Amen

Chapter
Thirty-Two

Jam'n Java
For the Soul

Book One

November 6

I wish to begin by giving you a one question quiz:

Today marks the death of one of the great military *rulers of the Reformation.*

Do you know who this man was?

His name is Gustavus Adolphus and it was due to his military prowess that Protestantism survived after the death of Luther.

He helped defend the Protestants, and particularly Lutheranism, when all the European religious wars broke out.

Anyway, it was Gustavus Adolphus Day in Sweden today.

And this has absolutely nothing to do with what I want to share with you.

- I've always had an interest in him and just thought he was a very important figure in the Reformation who is generally ignored or forgotten.

One of the things that concerns me as a Christian and a Pastor is the way so many people, even in the church, let fear govern their lives.

- *Have you noticed people who become terrified over what might happen?*
- *I'm not immune to this by any means.*
- *There are times when I get bogged down in fear and my thinking become focused around things like, "Well, what if this happens?"*
- *Or, "What if that happens? What will I do? What will my wife and I do?"*
- *Or "What will my children do?"*
- *This kind of thinking and concern can become a trap and plague us because once we give ourselves over to our fears, fear begins to control us.*

In 2 Timothy 1:7 St Paul writes, "God has given us a spirit, not of fear, but of power, of love, and of self-control."

- *When St Paul wrote those words he was literally a "prisoner for the Gospel"*
- *He was in Rome under house arrest awaiting trial before Caesar*
- *And he wrote those words to Timothy, his young protégée, who was a young and inexperienced Pastor*

Can you imagine what was going through Timothy's mind as he went about his daily duties?

- *I am sure he was concerned about Paul and whether he would survive his trial*
- *But he was probably concerned about his own life and what would happen to him and the people he was called to serve as Pastor*

From time-to-time, I've had people tell me something that has happened is the "worst possible thing" that could happen to them or their family

- *And I've often asked them, "Is it really? Is it really the 'worst possible thing?"*
- *I've told them, "It may be really bad, but can you think of anything worse that might happen?"*
- *Almost always they can.*

There isn't a single person who doesn't go through difficult or hard times.

- *Bad things do happen to good people*
- *Bad things happen to Christians, to people who love God*
- *Why?*
- *Because of sin, our own or the sin of others*
- *Or – just because!*
- *You and I have a choice in how we think about things*
- *We can let our fear control us and our thinking and actions*

-

- *Or we can realize what S.t Paul says:*
- *The spirit God has given us, placed within us through our faith and the work of His holy Spirit, is not one of fear, but of power*
- *The power that lies within the promises of God and the assurance of Romans 8 that nothing in all creation will be able to separate us from the love of God that is in Christ Jesus our Lord*

That same spirit is the spirit of love

- *Love that is our because He first loved us and gave His Son to die for us*

It is also the spirit of self-control

- *I probably need to reflect on that the next time I'm presented with a big piece of chocolate cake!*
- *Seriously though, it is something all of us need to remember when people around us give themselves over to the fear of what might happen*
- *Or what has happened, or what could happen*
- *Or, when we find ourselves focused on or fears and uncertainties*

A few verses after Paul writes this to Timothy he says:

- *I am not ashamed, for I know whom I have believed, and am convinced that he is able to guard until that day what has been entrusted to me.*
- *No matter what happens to us beloved, God is still in control*
- *And when bad things happen, as they will, it doesn't mean He is angry with us or no longer loves us*
- *It's just life and stuff is going to happen*
- *But it's also a life in which we have been given a spirit, not of fear, but of power, and love, and self-control*

Let's Pray:

Father in heaven, there is so much going on in this world that concerns us; things which sometimes seem to indicate that evil is in control.

There are so many places where war and hostility have erupted, and destruction and death seem to rule.

There are diseases that seem to run rampant with few solutions.

Governments seem to be breaking down and hatred seems to be on the rise.

And we don't always understand what is happening or why.

And in our weakness, we may wonder where You are, and why You don't do something about these things.

The answer to that question is You already have done something about all of this wickedness and evil – You sent Your only Son into this world and He took upon Himself all of this wickedness and evil and died for it. He offered His life to redeem this world, and us.

Father, help us to remember it is not what happens to us that is important, but how we respond to it. And we can respond in fear, or we can respond in faith and trust. We know You hold not only our life but also this world in Your hands.

And when we are in Your hands, we are safe, no matter what our experiences might tell us.

Assure us that You are with us in all things. Be with those who we lift up before You in our own hearts and minds tonight. In Jesus' name.

Amen

Chapter
Thirty-Three

Jam'n Java
For the Soul

Book One

November 13

One of the lessons for yesterday was from Paul's first letter to the Thessalonians, chapter 4:13-18, which reads as follows:

- *But we do not want you to be uninformed, brothers, about those who are asleep, that you may not grieve as others do who have no hope. [14] For since we believe that Jesus died and rose again, even so, through Jesus, God will bring with him those who have fallen asleep. [15] For this we declare to you by a word from the Lord, that we who are alive, who are left until the coming of the Lord, will not precede those who have fallen asleep. [16] For the Lord himself will descend from heaven with a cry of command, with the voice of an archangel, and with the sound of the trumpet of God. And the dead in Christ will rise first. [17] Then we who are alive, who are left, will be caught up together with them in the clouds to meet the Lord in the air, and so we will always be with the Lord. [18] Therefore encourage one another with these words.*

You may wonder why this would be one of the appointed lessons for this past Sunday. Death is not something we talk about very much in our society.

And as I write that I can think of several commercials for life insurance I've seen on television recently! But when's the last time you sat down with a group of friends over dinner and had a nice long discussion about death? That would be weird, right?

The reason this is one of the lessons for this past Sunday is that we are coming to the end of the Church year.

And what do we think about at the end of the year in our society? We think about the past year and maybe make some resolutions or goals for the coming year. But in the Church, we think not only about one year ending and another beginning, but we also think about the end of all things.

We think about the return of our Lord Jesus. And that's a subject many people either reject or just don't want to talk about.

The members of this congregation in Thessalonica had somehow **misunderstood** what St. Paul taught them about death and the end of all things. Somehow they had come to believe that it was necessary for believers to still be alive when Jesus returned for them, in order for them to be taken to heaven. Forgiveness of sins belongs to you.

And the disquieting implication of these thoughts was that their loved ones who had already died were not going to be in heaven with them.

I know this is probably so foreign to our way of thinking that it seems foolish to us. After all, our society seems to think everyone is going to heaven. Only the really bad people will be rejected and spend eternity in hell.

- **But we have to remember that these were people who had been steeped in paganism. Generally speaking, in the paganism of their day, death meant obliteration and oblivion. There was no hope, and no future for anyone. And so, the pagans grieved with despair.**

That's why St. Paul writes that we should not grieve as those who have no hope,

Christians grieve. We go through all the same emotions as any other human being at the death of a loved one. Except hopelessness.

We know those who have died believing in Jesus as their Lord and Savior have died "in Christ." St. Paul tells us in the book of Romans that if we die with Christ, we will be raised with him.

And he says in this letter to the Thessalonians that the dead in Christ will rise first, and then the rest of us will be united with Him. This is comforting because we know that death is not the final word!

As I conclude, I know some of you may be thinking, "Well, this is a real downer!"

But let me remind all of us, me included, about how consistent this is with the whole Gospel. Psychologists have pointed out the many ways we grieve over things in life.

We don't just grieve over physical death, but the "death" of lost relationships such as a divorce. We may grieve over the loss of our health, or financial failures that we experience.

Remember what St. Paul writes in Romans 8, that there is nothing in this life, or even in death, that can separate us from the love of God that is ours through our Lord Jesus Christ.

Even though we go through many difficult things in life, we do not do so hopelessly. For we know that all things work together for good because of God's love and promise to us. And ultimately, at the end, we find a new beginning, in Christ.

Some things to think about:

This is a tough question, but have you talked about your own death with the person or people closest to you?

_____

_____

_____

Is it possible to live every day "ready to die" and yet eager to face the challenges and opportunities "tomorrow" might bring?

_____

_____

_____

Does it seem "morbid" to spend some time talking with others about death?

_____

_____

_____

While Christians are not "eager" to die, they can be ready to do so at any moment. Does that seem impossible to You?

Let's Pray:

Father in heaven, thank you for the love that overcomes our darkest hours and days.

Thank you for the hope that is ours through our Lord Jesus which lifts us out of the deep gloom and despair that is so common in this world. Be with those who are suffering loss and grieving tonight.

Wrap Your arms of love and compassion around them and give them hope.

We pray for those who are undergoing medical procedures or soon will be. And pray for their healing. Guide and bless the physicians and medical personnel who minister to them.

We serve and glorify You in all that we do. In Jesus' name.

Amen

Chapter
Thirty-Four

Jam'n Java
For the Soul

Book One

November 20

As I write this, we are already in Thanksgiving week. Time just seems to be flying by!

I'd like to share a couple of thoughts with you based on Matthew 25:14-30.

I'm not going to print the whole passage, but you are free to look it up. You probably know this passage as the parable of the talents.

Jesus is in the process of answering a question his disciples ask about the end of the world.

His answer begins in chapter 24 and continues into chapter 25. He tells four parables to answer their question.

- The parable of the fig tree
- The parable of the 10 virgins or young women
- This parable, the parable of the talents, and the parable of the sheep and the goats.

Briefly, the parable of the talents goes like this: There is a master who calls in three of his servants. He gives each one of them a gift, a very large sum of money.

To the first one he gives 5 talents, to the second servant three, and to the third, he gives one talent.

After doing this he leaves to take care of some business in a distant land. He does so without giving them any instructions.

We could make the argument that he didn't have to give them instructions because they knew what was expected of them as his servants.

But to understand this a little better, let's define how much money a talent was in those days.

To say that it was a very large sum of money is an understatement. It was the equivalent of 20 years' salary. Or maybe it's more understandable to say it was the working wage for one person over 20 years.

To put it into a context of our own society, the US government reported that the average salary in the US in 2022 was $60 thousand dollars.

Of course, some made more, some made less, but let's just work with that figure.

Using the figure of sixty thousand dollars a year, one talent would be the equivalent of one million, two hundred thousand dollars.

Five talents would be the equivalent of two million, four hundred thousand dollars. And ten talents would be the equivalent of million dollars. So, whether it is one five or ten talents we are talking about a very significant amount of money.

You know the story. When the master returns, he calls his servants in to see what they have accomplished. The first two have doubled his gift. One talent has been turned into four, and five talents have been turned into ten. But the third servant did nothing with the talent and gave it back to the master.

Obviously, I don't have enough time to develop the whole story and explain the background but let me say this: This parable is often used to talk to us about how we as Christians should be using the gifts God has given us.

I think that's a valid interpretation. But there is something else here that is equally important: this is a story about the graciousness of the master.

We are told that the Master gave these servants gifts "according to their abilities."

In other words, he had an intimate knowledge of them. He knew their strengths and weaknesses.

He knew where they would succeed and where they would fail.

And in gifting them accordingly, he set them up for success, not for failure. That is a point you and I need to hear over-and-over again.

The master gives these three servants a great gift. They have neither earned this gift nor do they deserve it. And that is just like our faith.

Let me just get to the point here: the greatest gift God has given each of us is our faith. We neither deserve it nor can earn it. It is simply His gift. Period.

This is the whole point of the Gospel.

Our faith, our relationship to God is all about what God has done for us, not what we can or should do for God. He has given us this gift that is beyond anything we can imagine and that is our faith.

It is our faith that sustains us during the hard times of life. It is our faith that reminds us that Jesus Christ lived a perfect life for us that we could never live for ourselves.

Let me put it this way: Jesus lived perfectly, *for you!* He died *for you!* He rose again *for you!* The forgiveness of sins belongs, *to you!*

And God has made you his own through baptism and the work of the holy spirit. He has done all of this – **for you!** Just so you could be his own and live with Him in His kingdom.

Some things to think about:

Excluding your faith and relationship to your Lord, what is the "greatest gift" you have ever been given?

_____

_____

Have you ever been given a gift by someone and didn't want to accept it because you thought the giver "couldn't afford" it?

_____

_____

From a purely human perspective, it could be argued that Jesus "couldn't afford" to do what He did for us.

But from another perspective, it might be argued that because of His love, He "couldn't afford" NOT to do what He did for us!

Let's Pray:

Father, thank You for all that You have done for us.

Thank You for the forgiveness of sins, the new life that we have through Jesus, and the tremendous gift of our faith which you have given us. Help us to use our faith and all Your gifts in ways that will glorify You.

Hear the cries of our hearts for those who are ill or going through difficult times.

Guide the doctors and nurses who minister to those we love. May all we do glorify You. In Jesus' name.

Amen

Chapter
Thirty-Five

Jam'n Java
For the Soul

Book One

December 4

I would like to share a thought or two with you based on 1 Corinthians 1:3-9. But I want to focus on verses 7-9 where St Paul writes:

"...you are not lacking in any gift as you await the revealing of our Lord Jesus Christ, who will sustain you to the end, guiltless in the day of our Lord Jesus Christ. God is faithful, by whom we were called into the fellowship of his Son, Jesus Christ."

If you know anything about the congregation in Corinth, it was a mess.

There was infighting, controversy, divisions and the kind of immorality that would shock many of us today. And St. Paul had to take them to task. But look where he begins his letter, with their relationship to the Lord Jesus Christ.

Without getting into any of the things that were going on in the congregation at Corinth, let's think about what's going on in our lives today.

We're in December, in the season of Advent, and we're getting prepared for Christmas. And that means our schedule is going to get filled with more things to get done and our lives will get more hectic every day until the season is over.

Are you one of those people who beat yourselves up over what you didn't get done? I am, to some extent. I can always find things I should have or could have done.

I think it's important to focus on what St. Paul writes in these verses, not just at this time of year, but all through the year, **Jesus Christ will sustain you to the end...**Not just the end of the Christmas season, but the end of the day, the end of the week, the end of the month, the end of the year, and the end of our lives.

It can be really easy to get down on ourselves, and find fault with ourselves, especially if some of those around us are pointing out our failures and inconsistencies.

I can look back on my life and wish I had done some things better; been a better Father, a better husband, a better son, and a better Pastor.

Well, who among us can't do that?

What St. Paul is pointing us to is not our failures or inconsistencies, but the faithfulness of God, who sustains us every day, and at the end. When you and I think we're going to get hammered by God for all our failures, we find instead, in Christ Jesus, we are guiltless before God.

All the things we beat ourselves up over, or find fault within ourselves for, don't really matter, because before God, through Jesus, we are guiltless. Because it's not about you or me, it's about God, and what He has done for us, in Christ Jesus.

I love this time of year, but not for the presents or the special services, and gatherings. I love all those things, but more important, I see in the star above the manger - the shadow of the cross - this child who came will come again, and with Him comes our salvation.

Some things to think about:

Considering all the things we have done in the past, all our weaknesses and failures, how can God see us as "**guiltless in the day of our Lord Jesus Christ**" (the Last day)? The good news of the Gospel is that *"God is faithful"* and He will bring it about for you – no matter what – salvation is ours in Christ Jesus.

Let's Pray:

Father in Heaven, thank You for the gift of Your love that sustains us every day even though there are times we don't recognize it. We often focus only on things that show us our failures, our shortcomings, or our sins.

Help us to see in the Babe of Bethlehem Your faithfulness to us. It is so easy, Father, to focus on the daily struggles, the problems and the difficulties we have.

Help us to recognize Your grace which is sufficient for every need we have each and every day of our lives. In Jesus' precious name.

Amen

Chapter
Thirty-Six

JaM'n Java
For the Soul
Book One

December 11

I'd like to share a couple of thoughts with you based on Romans 15:15

- ***May the God of Hope fill you with all joy and peace in believing, so that by the power of the Holy Spirit you may abound in hope.***

During the Advent season we talk a lot about the love of God as well as peace.

After all, a part of the angels' message to the shepherds was, ***"Peace on earth, good will to men."***

And we all know John 3:16 "***God so loved the world that he gave his only begotten son that whosoever believes in him will not perish but have everlasting life.***

But maybe we should also think about the fact that our God is the God of Hope, as St. Paul calls him.

Life can be difficult, no matter what season of the year we are in. But this season, the season of Christmas, can be especially rough for people who find themselves alone. Some people wonder what there is to feel joyful about.

The sad truth is at this time of year more suicides are committed than any other.

Maybe they have no family or friends to gather with. Or maybe the death of a loved one has caused an extreme feeling of loneliness and isolation. They might be experiencing sickness and illness. Maybe they are experiencing some kind of bitterness or resentment which has festered and grown into separation.

There's a commercial I've seen more than once that talks about this sort of thing, but it places the blame on arguments that have arisen in past years within family groups. It encourages conversation and acceptance of others' opinions.

That helps, but it's not the ultimate answer. The ultimate answer is found in the God of Hope, who, as St. Paul says, *fills us with all joy and peace in believing...*In other words, it is the God of hope who has given us the gift of faith, who fills us with joy and peace, so that through the power of the Holy Spirit we may abound in hope.

The lyrics for one of my favorite hymns growing up said this:

My hope is built on nothing less than Jesus' blood and righteousness.

No merit of my own, I claim, but whole lean on Jesus' name. On Christ the solid rock I stand, all other ground is sinking sand.

Our God is the God of Hope: The God of Hope, not the God of gloom and doom. He is the God of Hope, not the God of despair or doubt.

The God of Hope, not the God of anger and vengeance. The God who, as St Peter says, *is patient, and would have all men to be saved*. The God who has no logical reason to love us but does anyway.

The God who sees our needs, our loneliness, our pain and our isolation, and doesn't ignore those factors in our lives, but comes in the person of His Son to meet them and supply all we need and more. He is the God who fills us with joy and peace, through our faith. And hope.

Some things to think about:

How is God the "God of Hope" even when things are difficult, or we struggle with the circumstances or situations of life? Hope is not some kind of "belief" that "behind every cloud is a silver lining," but in the end, no matter what happens, the victory is ours because of the promise of God says so.

Let's Pray:

Father in heaven, we thank You for Your love and mercy.

We ask You this evening to help us to reach out to those who are lonely or isolated, those who feel abandoned and may have no hope.

Use us to love them in such a way that they are surrounded by Your love, and in that love, may they find joy and peace, and hope.

Fill our lives with the hope that You alone can give as we live each day with lives that are built on Christ, the solid rock. May we stand on Him alone. In Jesus' name.

Amen

Chapter
Thirty-Seven

Jam'n Java
For the Soul
Book One

December 18

I was thinking about how busy I'm going to be this week; Jam' n Java tonight, the annual Jam For Jesus Concert with Robby Robinson and Friends, tomorrow night, Wednesday Advent Services, Thursday Choir practice, a family gathering on Saturday, and, by the way, my sister is coming in to stay with us tomorrow.

And your schedule is probably just as busy as mine. It's one of the things about this time of year that makes us focus on all the things we have to do instead of what this season is all about. It's also probably what wears us out and makes us feel like we need a vacation afterwards.

- In Luke 2 we're told that when the shepherds visited Mary and Joseph and told them about what the angels had said, Mary *"treasured all these things, pondering them in her heart."*

Wouldn't we be wondering about all this stuff too?

First there's the angel that tells Mary she's going to give birth to the Lord's anointed. Then she goes off to stay with her cousin Elizabeth, who is pregnant with John the Baptizer.

I'm guessing she's there about three months and returns home, and that's when things really break lose. It's discovered that she's pregnant. Can you imagine her father's reaction? Can you imagine the sense of shame he must have felt as he broke the news to Joseph that Mary was pregnant!

Joseph could have divorced her publicly, and put her to shame, even going so far as to have her stoned to death. But he decided to do it quietly so she wouldn't be shamed publicly. And then the angel appears to Joseph and tells him everything is okay, Mary hasn't been irresponsible or unfaithful – this is of God.

So, then they get married, and she's what; three or four months along? They're probably going through all the struggles newlyweds have, getting used to having each other around all the time, and adjusting to their new situation. It's not easy under normal circumstance and their circumstances were anything but normal!

And then there's this Roman Emperor who decides he wants to know how many people are in the kingdom – for tax purposes of course – and they are forced to walk to Bethlehem about the time she's supposed to deliver.

There's no **Motel 6** or **Holiday Inn** and the only place they can find shelter is at a stable filled with farm animals with a manger – and that's where the Savior of the world is born.

And the same night, there's these shepherds who come and find them and tell them this strange story about angels and praising God. And if that's not enough, the shepherds go around telling everybody in Bethlehem about it!

No wonder she's taking some time to think and reflect, to treasure these things, and to try to figure out what it all means.

You and I have the benefit of hindsight. We know what it all means. The Apostle Paul writes in Romans 5, *"…at the right time Christ died for the ungodly…God shows His love for us in that while we were still sinners, Christ died for us."*

But we still live in the tension of knowing what it's all about, but still living out our day to day lives trying to put it all together.

I guess what I trying to say is this: no matter how hectic it gets during these days ahead, or for the rest of our lives, for that matter, take some time to pause and reflect on this: what we see here is God's plan of salvation coming to fruition.

God incarnate, visible, in the flesh comes into this world for one reason only, to redeem the lost and condemned people – people like you and me.

God incarnate, in the flesh, the visible expression of the love of God for you – and for me.

And that's what this season is all about…

The love of God – for you.

The gift of God – for you.

The salvation of God – for you.

Some things to think about:

Christ not only came "at the right time" in the history of the world, but He also comes "in the right time" for each of us; when things are difficult or uncertain, when we struggle or are filled with fear. In this "hurry scurry" world we live in, He is with us and beside us, "at the right time."

Let's Pray:

Father in heaven help us to keep from getting caught up in all the things we have to do at this time of year and help us to pause and reflect; to ponder and treasure up Your love for us.

Help us to remember that all the tinsel and wrapping paper, the food and celebration, are there to remind us of the great love you have for us.

May we return Your love for us by loving one another. And may we focus on the greatest gift we will ever receive – eternal life and salvation won for us through Your Son, Jesus Christ.

Hear the cries of our hearts on behalf of those who are injured or sick, who are going through difficult times and struggling in their various situations or circumstances.

May they, and we, find our peace in You. In Jesus' name.

Amen

No Gift Wrapped Beneath
The Christmas Tree
Will Ever Compare to the
Gift God Gave to You and Me

- K.P. Lynne

Meet the Author

C.W. Pearson
"Pastor Chuck"

Pastor Chuck appears weekly on *Jam' n Java*, a popular internet broadcast, hosted by #1 Hypeddit Recording Artist, Hammond® Organ aficionado, keyboard player and music director for Frankie Valli and the Four Seasons, **Robby Robinson.**

Pastor Chuck serves as *Jam' n Java's* official on-air chaplain. Every Monday night, **Pastor Chuck** touches countless lives, nationally and globally, via his **Christian** devotionals, preaching the *Word of the Lord*, seasoned with his own heavenly insight, original prayers and down-to-earth words of wisdom.

As an author, **Pastor Chuck** collaborates with a much **"higher power"** and dedicates his creative endeavors to his co-author, **Jesus Christ**, whose **"Words"** are the cornerstone of his books. All glory goes to **Jesus Christ,** who holds **Pastor Chuck's** pen, and inspires his creative writing.

A multitalented gentleman, blessed with an abundance of gifts, **Pastor Chuck** is currently working on *Jam' n Java For the Soul: Book Two*, as well as fictional works for youth and adults.

Pastor Chuck holds a **Bachelor of Divinity** from **Concordia Theological Seminary** and a **Music Education** degree from **Western State University**.

Pastor Chuck plays the trumpet, writes songs, and creates visual artwork. His crowning glory is a 6-foot x 9-foot stained-glass cross which adorns the outer entrance to **Trinity Lutheran Church** in **Simi Valley, California**. **Pastor Chuck's** religious and secular creations are available on a smaller scale at **GodsGlassStudio** on **Etsy**.

Pastor Chuck takes every opportunity to be a faithful shepherd and gives of himself as a volunteer. He dutifully serves as a community leader, role model, mentor, choir member, bible study facilitator and worship leader. **Pastor Chuck** is on the Board of Directors as the Director of Spiritual Life at **Trinity Lutheran Church in Simi Valley**.

Robby Robinson
RobbysRecords.com

If You Love Music and Faith
You'll Love Jam' n Java

Hosted By Robby Robinson

#1 Hypeddit® Recording Artist, Hammond® Organ Endorsed Keyboard Artist
Music Director and Keyboard Player for Frankie Valli and the Four Seasons

Streaming Worldwide

Every Monday

7 p.m. Pacific, 9 p.m. Central, 10 p.m. Eastern

You Tube

www.youtube.com/JamnJava

facebook

www.facebook.com/jamnjava

Trinity Lutheran Church
Simi Valley, California

Photo By C.W. Pearson

Rev. Robert Lyon Barker, Senior Pastor
www.TrinityLutheranChurchSimi.com